Introduction to
MAYANS' TREATISE ON
ASTRONOMY

Introduction to
MAYANS' TREATISE ON
ASTRONOMY

M.R.SOWRIRAJAN

"God's Own Ring".

PARTRIDGE
A Penguin Random House Company

To order additional copies of this book, contact
Partridge India
000 800 10062 62
orders.india@partridgepublishing.com

www.partridgepublishing.com/india

CONTENTS

PREFACE

Vall(h)uvam is the ancient treatise in Tamil on Astronomy duly computed and codified. Those, who were well educated and trained as technocrats, are declared as Mayans, and also as Maya Aryans in Tamil. They are referred to as Paramacharya Mayan in Sanskrit Compilation, Srimad Bhagavatham.

Thamizh (Tamil), as the proper name of this Language, and will hereafter be referred to as such.

Those, who are well educated in Vall(h)uvam, established by Mayans of ancient period, and trained in computing time. Day, date, year, etc., are declared as Vall(h)vars. Even today there are very many of them practicing in Tamizh Nadu (Tamil Nadu -South India). But unfortunately, they are not recognized / encouraged, and also treated as backward in Social Order. Over and above this, there have been efforts in recent times to bulldoze this great scientific treatise by certain zealots. Some of the terms on this subject are as follows:

Computation of Year is based on, 1) Parivaccharam –Traverse of the Earth around Sun on its own Trajectory, termed Parivattom: 2) Anuvaccharam- Traverse of the Moon around the Earth, under the axial control of the Earth; and 3) Idavaccharam- Earth's rotation on its own axis (rotation of Earth's surface, enabling computation of time and day).

All the above three are computed together and termed as Samvaccharam. The year so computed is termed as "Samvacchara Aandu" (Aandu --Year).

Earth's inclination is established as 22-1/2 thithi's ('Thithi' denotes 'degree'). Details on this is clarified in the text under 'Star'.

Since Earth is traversing around Sun in spiraling pattern, Earth is slowly drifting, and, therefore, number of days of Samvaccharam year increases by one second for every 20 years. Details of this are furnished in the main Text.

Earth's Equator is termed Visuvathanam, in which, 'Visu' refers to oscillation, i.e., Beam of Sun light oscillates between Northern and Southern hemispheres.

The first day of the year, i.e., 1st of Chithirai, during which the beam of Sunlight falls evenly on both the hemispheres.

The Almanac of Samvacchara year is termed as 'Kaala Thiruk kanitham' Even this has been altered today as Thiruk kanitha Panchankam after 2nd Century A.D., by the migrants(Cherars), who occupied in groups in forests initially and later spread out in the Southern states.

There are Vall(h)uvars, devoted to this great science and strictly follow the procedures for computing the 'kaala thiruk kanitham'. But instead of encouraging them they are treated as backward in the Society. Now, of late, efforts are made to do away with Val(h)uvam once and for all by certain Zealots under the guise of Rationalism, that too in the land in which Mayans evolved, studied and established Vall(h)uvam as Aaya kalai (Treatise).

This book is written to introduce Vall(h)uvam, the Mayan Treatise on Astronomy, with historical notes, wherever necessary.

Salient features of the Book: "Introduction to Mayans' Treatise on Astronomy".

It is mentioned in Ancient Thamizh history that there were 64 Aaya Kalais (Treatises) preserved in the 'Thamizh Literary Association' [Thamizh Chankam], and that, they were submerged in the Sea during a Catastrophe, which rocked the world about 5,100 years ago. But, it was the practice in those days to hear and grasp those treatises in their memories. These great scholars used to impart these treatises to their disciples, step by step, along with practical training, which is still in vogue.[Tamil is a phonetic variant of Thamizh]

This Book is written and documented on Ancient 'Vall(h) uvam' — Astronomy'. This book also contains historical notes, wherever necessary. (P.S.: 'h' in bracket implies that the previous alphabet is to be pronounced by turning the tongue inwardly and express a bit hard. This applies to 'l' and 'n' alphabets).

Sources:

1) For three years, (1947-50), learnt methodically under a

   Septuagenarian Vall(h)uvar, following the ancient methodology, viz., the teacher would impart step by step and the desciple had to grasp subject and memorize.

2) Learnt "Tri-fold great Truths," a simple way of learning, Evolution from the Core of Nature, Formation of Universe, and Evolution of Basic Particles (Vasu in Thamizh), etc., from my father, (Late) M.S.Ramanujachari, of 'Madapusi-Seat of Higher Learning.'(Tamil is a phonetic variant of Thamizh. In this book, the nomenclature, 'Thamizh only is used)

3) Thamizh (generally known as Tamil) Pallaandu Psalms rendered by Periyazhwar (4th/3rd B.C.).

4) **3rd** to **9th** Cantos (Sections), of Shrimad Bhagavatham, compilation of all the scriptures and history by three Yetis, i.e., 1) Vyasar, known as Veda Vyasar, 2) Maithreya, and 3) Sukha, and rendered by Sukha, during the Catastrophe, which rocked the world about 5,100 ago.

5) Lord Krishna's Revelations to Arjuna – Shrimad Bhaghavad Geetha.

Please Note: All the nomenclatures in this Book pertain to Astro - Physical Terms, which are properly defined. These have no reference or relationship to the same or similar names found in 'Scriptures' of various Religious Schools of thought.

M.R. Sowrirajan, Author.

CHAPTER 1

Mayans' Treatise on Astronomy - Vallhuvam

NOTES ON ANCIENT INDIA:

The country, now referred to as India, was called "Thiruvidam", (Thamizh nomenclature) in ancient times. Thiru is the first syllable of Thiruttham, meaning 'Blemish less'. The same word, while referring to the Core of Nature, means 'Absolute'. In Paali language/ Sanskrit this country was called 'Dravidam', a Phonetic variant of the Thamizh word. This name was later translated into Sanskrit as 'Punitha Bhoomi', meaning Holy Land.

The northern mountain Range was termed 'Imaya kootam'. Imai refers to eyelid and kootam –congregation. As the mountain Range, situated in the north of this country, is similar to the eye lid, it was called as such. It was referred to as Hema kootam, a phonetic variant, and further, some misinterpreted in Sanskrit that 'Hema' meant 'Gold'.(The actual Sanskrit word for Gold is swarnam). Some other sections again twisted the name to suit their schism, as Himalaya, in which, according to them, Hima refers to snow. The actual word for snow is 'sisiram' ('s' is pronounced midway between s and sh).

Later, the name of this mountain range was translated into Sanskrit as 'Nethra Paalam', [Nethra – eye and paalam - nurture and protect) which refers to eyelid], and was later referred in short form, as Nepalam. Today, there is a country by the name, '**Nepal**', situated on this mountain range.

When the world was struck by catastrophe, three Yetis, (Yathis) Krishna Dwaipayana, known as Veda Vyasa, Maithreya, and Suka, left Naimisa Aranya, their abode on the Bank of Gomati River, on the slope of Imayam,

(North of Lucknow) and reached Badarika Ashrama (Today known as Bhadrinath). There, on the advice of Shoodra Acharya, Naratha, compiled all the Puranas, Upanishaths, historical details, Social life of various countries of Asia, and brought out Shrimad Bhagavatham, consisting of 18 Cantos. Krishna Dwaipayana left the mortal world after narrating the first two cantos and Maithreya left the mortal world after narrating 3rd to 5th canto. Suka recorded all the 18 cantos, left Badarika Ashrama and went to Hasthinapura.

As earth tremors started rocking the areas along Imayam, Parikshit, the King of Hastinapura, and courtiers left their dwellings and assembled at the open area on the bank of the nearby river. When Suka reached there, another Yeti, Sootha, introduced him to the King and informed that Suka would narrate Shrimad Bhagavatham. When Suka completed narration of the 8th Canto consisting of Soma Purana (Soma – God of Moon), and Soma Vamsis (People following Lunar Calendar, living in Mongolia, China and middle East), Parikshit requested him to narrate on Vivasvaan, and those ten born to him, "Vaivasvatha Man" as the first and "Ikshvaaku", the noteworthy.

Then Suka commenced narration of 9th Canto -Dravida Vamsha – People belonging to Thiruvidam. At the outset he told, "Oh King, to narrate on Dravida Vamsha, even hundred years would not suffice. I shall narrate a few of them". So saying, he started the narration. Dravidians were destined to be shoodhras. They lived with what they earned out of their professions (toil). They never accepted anything as Dana (Gratis) from others. They had great aptitude for gaining knowledge and training. Then he commenced with their findings on Evolution of Life System onwards."

Theories and great truths derived and established by Dravidians on various fields of knowledge are praiseworthy. These were declared as Aaya Kalai, meaning 'Treatises'. It was mentioned in Thamizh history that there were 64 Aaya Kalai's.

Mathura city was built by the King, Pandyan Malayavaan, where the first Thamizh Chankam, known as Thalai Chankam (pronounced as Sankam), i.e.,

Thamizh Literary Association, was instituted by Ahkatiyar about 7,500 years ago. This was in vogue for about 500 years and became inactive due to natural calamity. Again, Second Thamizh Chankam was instituted about 5,500 years ago at Mathura, which was in vogue for about 300 years.

During the catastrophe, that rocked the world, very many Volcanoes erupted, spilling lava into the oceans and seas, thereby Ice Bergs melted and sea water level rose. Mathura City, built by Pandian Malayavaan, was submerged into sea, along with all documents, and various literary works collected and preserved in Thamizh chankam(Both 1st 2nd).

In spite of it, very many Specialists and Professionals zealously learnt them, preserved and practiced. Among them are various scientific and technical Treatises, known as Maya Aaya kalai. Those Dravidians, who were Scientists and Technocrats were declared as Mayans. The day and time line: Mayans marked the line at a point on Visuvatham relating to 90 degrees Meridian, as Day Break (time 'o'- relating to 6A.M.) on Kandava Vana.

Kandava vana – This island was long like sugarcane, commencing about a few hundred Kilometers south of Bengal coast, west of Andaman and extended down south, slightly bent at Visuvathanam-Equator, westward, and extended far South. Shallow landscape linked it with Makara Theevu (Australian island), and another, linked it with Aati Island (Antarctica island). One more island existed linking several islands south and east of Makara theevu (Australia).

(Aati –glass; The Island, covered with Ice, looked like glass).

Makara – The one that keeps its mouth open, when on earth. This refers to huge crocodiles of ancient period. As this island is noted for this species, it was called as such).

Andaman and Nicobar were long landscapes linked to Kandava vana, just as branches of Deer-horn, what is today called Sumatra, Jawa, etc. islands were also linked as a long landscape, extending to far-east. Further, Borneo, and also Madura islands were contiguous part like branches of Deer horn. These were also termed as Mankombuth theevu.

It was mentioned that there were eight powerful volcanoes in this island Ranges.

During the catastrophe all the volcanoes in Kandava vana erupted, practically bringing down major part of it. The sea level also arose in this catastrophe, drowning the shallow lands and plains, resulting in the plateaus and hills remain as islands as we find them today.

Mathura city was submerged into sea, and the platue is left as a small island, north east of Jawa.

[Note: Earlier name of Malaysia was Malaya. Though the name of the country has changed, the people of this country are referred to as Malays and their Language as Malaay. This name denotes the area ruled by Pandyan Malayavan.]

As part of ancient history, mentioned by Shoodra Acharya (Professor) Naratha to king Ashwajith (about 8,000 years ago (Shrimad Bhagavatham) that (females were less in those days, i.e., 12,500 years ago) Pandian Malayavan fought and won a woman and took her as his wife. They had eight sons, to whom he bequeathed the areas, he ruled, as eight Dravida Desams (desam-country), and retired to a place, at Kula Aalam, Chandra vaahi, and Thambra Bharani (River), and spent the rest of his life, fixing his mind in Shriman Narayana.

[Kula Aalam –Kutralam as known today; Aalam is Banyan tree, and during the course of time most part of this tree had been cut off and only a small portion is left out as a memento. Even in this case the cherars (migrants) have fabricated fictitious stories to suit their schisms.

Chandra vaahi- Chandra- sound reverberation and vaahi the one that carries, and, as such, it refers to a curved portion of the mountain that echoes; Thambra Bharani river, which flows along this mountain Range southwards. The place referred to by Naratha is the town known as Seervilliputhur (Srivilliputhur, as it is called today). Here, the Lord is reclining on the Banyan leaf, and referred to in Thamizh as Aalilai Kidanthaan, and Vatapathra Sayee in Sanskrit. Vata vriksham is the Sanskrit term for Aala Maram (Banyan Tree).

Mathurai – (known as Mathura/Madura) It is of two syllables: - Math and Urai. Math – 'ma' refers to mind (self) 'th'-root/source of knowledge, and as such it means, the root of knowledge embedded in mind; urai –reveal through expression (speech). The word thus implies that, this place is the source of knowledge and language (expression).]

This was the town, where, about 7,500 years ago, Ahkatthiyar (pronounced as Ahatthiyar) devoting his life for the language Thamizh, compiled all important portions of ancient documents, set Grammer, codified the language into three parts, viz., Iyal-Prosaic, Isai –Music as Chandam(vocal controls), Mettu (Octaves), and pan(h) (Musical notes), and Natakam –dramatics and dance. He titled his compilation as "Thol Kappiyam- Documentation based on ancient literary works. For this magnificient work, he was glorified as 'Tholkaapiyan'. Dedicating this document, he instituted the first Thamizh Chankam, known as Thalai Chankam-the prime literary Association. Thiruvalluvar Perunthahai, in his Dedication to his Epic- Thirukkural, refers to the language as "Kuru Munivan Thamizh"., implying the language as instituted by Ahatthiyar.

(Kuru- code of life; munivan- the one who takes responsibility upon himself, puts his effort, and performs as his duty).

History of Mathura in the North (about 40 kilometers south of Delhi.):-

Rama was enthroned at Ayodhya. Since it was mentioned that Ahatthiyar was present in the Coronation, Rama's period was also 7,500 years ago. (9th Canto of Srimad Bhagavatham, deals with Dravida vamsa).

[Note: Dravida - Phonetic variant of Thamizh- Thiruvidam, i.e., Blemishless land, and Dravida vamsa,.i.e., Dravidians – natives of Thiruvidam).

From 9th chapter onwards Rama's history was furnished in brief, which only reveals that Rama was a Dravidian and also Shoodra and not Kshatria of Soma vamsa Manu vaadam

In brief, Rama in due course, enthroned Kucha, second of the twin sons, accepting the fact that the one born second is the elder, and the first born is younger. After this he left Ayodhya crossing the river Sarayu, for Badarikaashrama. While leaving, he directed Lakshmana to go to 'Kapila Teertha', at the confluence of Ganga and Sea (Bay of Bengal). 144 names as lineage of Rama were mentioned in the 9th Canto and all were renowned kings and Charioteers as well. The 144th named Bruhath Paala, fought in Mahabharata war on the side of Dhuryodhana, and was killed by Abhimanyu, Charioteer and son of Arjuna. With him the Rule of Rama's lineage at Ayodhya ended., that was about 2,500 years after Rama.]

While his step Brother Lakshmana stayed with Rama and assisted him in his rule of the country. Bharatha, another Step brother. left for Kekaya kingdom. Since his maternal uncle did not have male progeny, Bharatha became the king of that kingdom.

(Lord Buddha was from the lineage of Bharatha. He mentions this to Ambatta, a Brahmin youth, who came to meet him in Buddha Vihara in Icchalananka forest-Kosala Kingdom, thus: My ancestor, Ikshvaku king, wishing to enthrone the son of his second wife, banished all his four sons. He mentioned this indirectly, since Lord Rama was already deified as God incarnate, which not only separated him from the hearts of people, but also was devoid of truth, he did not want himself to be deified as God incarnate, as this would separate him from the people for whom he had devoted his life to redeem them from miseries caused by the rulers and their coteries.-Ref:-"Ambatta Suttha").

Shathrugna, twin brother of Lakshmana, who was always with Bharatha, left him, cleared the forest on the western bank of Kaaliya River (Today known as Yamuna river), built a city, and named it 'Mathura', after the city Mathurai built by his ancestor Pandiyan Malayavaan.

[Kaaliya River –Kaala- Time; this name indicates the river of ancient times

While this city was built on the west bank, there was already a township called Aayarpaadi, Aravam language, the second stage of evolution of Thamizh language after the advent of introduction of 'Kol Ezhuthu'(stroke alphabets) enabling writing down documents, It was 'Vaimozhi, i.e., spoken language till then.. It was referred to in Mahabharata as Gokulam (phonetic variant of Thamizh word – Kokulam), which refers to the sect of the people lived there. Sanskrit version of this is Varshaneeya Kulam. They are from the lineage of Dhruva (phonetic variant of Thamizh name – Thiruvan). Lord Krishna was from this lineage, and was glorified as Vaarshaneeyah, meaning, the jewel of the lineage.]

The lineage of Shatrugna was called "Bhoja". (Bho- phonetic variant of Thamizh 'Po', the first alphabet of the word 'Potruthal'-praiseworthy; ja- first syllable of Jana, i.e., people.

Bhoja as Dynasty ruled up to 12th Century A.D.. Highly enlightened as they were, were loved by people of the Kingdom. Note worthy is Vikramadithya –I, Learned and righteous, his rule was glorious, such that, after his demise, an Era, based on Samvacchara calendar (to be dealt with in the Text), viz., Vikrama Samvacchara commenced. After him Vikramadithya-II was equally glorified a Bhoja Raja (Jewel of the dynasty). He decorated his Royal Court with nine learned scholars of different fields, noteworthy of them are, 1) Ariya Pattan –who introduced Decimal system, Logarithm and Algebra; 2) Varahamihira-Astronomer; 3) Dhanwanthari –Physician; 4) Paanini, Musician; 5) Maghah-Poet and Lyricist, and 6) Kaalidasa, the renowned, Composer of Epic-Plays.

Various stories were written Vikramadithya-I and II, merely out of jealousy and intolerance by certain Protagonists of Manuvaada Varnaasrama, as they were Dravidians, who never practiced nor entertained Caste System by birth.

The same was the case of Kaalidasa also. Kaalidasa was his pen name, which refers to the hoary culture of those lived in the past along this River, and he was an obedient subject of them. (Kaali – the river, and dasa-obedient subject/servant).

Vikramadhithya-II built a city, south of Mathura, as the central place of his Kingdom, and named I Bhojapala puri, which is shortened and called 'Bhopal' today.

<u>Present Mathurai in South India</u>: First Thamizh Chankam instituted about 7,500 years ago, ceased to function after about 500 years due to natural calamities. Then the second Chankam instituted about 5,500 years ago, also became defunct after 300 years due to the catastrophe that rocked the world. Thereafter, a Pandya King built a city on the Eastern Bank of Vaigai River (In Tamil Nadu) and revived ThamizhChankam. As this was the last Chankam for promoting Thamizh language and literature, it was called "Kadai chankam". (Kadai -The last one). On the Western Bank was the ancient city named "Koodal Nakaram". This Mathurai was burnt down after 250 years, and the Kadai chankam also became defunct. Thereafter, the Cherars (migrants) started calling Koodal Nakaram as Mathurai, and also wrote stories, to suit their own schisms.

Note.- Kandava vana was submerged in the month of Aati-Avani (month of August) on a Full Moon day, and Thiru Onam star On this day every year, the learned in the South go to the sea shore of Bay of Bengal and do Tharpana (ritual owing their knowledge to the great seers lived in that island). Thereafter Kaliyuka commenced. Today we are living in the year Kaliyuka 5,114 (2012-13). In Kandava vana, at a point relating to 90 degrees East, Meridian, Mayans constructed Circular Time chamber (Nazhikai Vattil. (Naazhikai-Unit time, equivalent to 24 minutes, Vattil- circular chamber). As this was also submerged, a fresh Naazhikai Vattil was constructed in Thiru Arangan Temple (Ranganatha temple, as is now known) in Thamizh nadu (Tamil nadu), and Vall(h)uvars continued their pursuit of Astronomy.

In 2nd Century A.D. Yakshas (Konkars), declaring themselves as Vaishnavites, who came along with kalappirars (Kapalikas) spread out in the Southern parts, took control of this temple with the help of kalappirars, drove away all the Tamizh priests and also Vall(h)uvars. Then they declared that Sanskrit was the Language of Devas, and introduced Sanskrit as the only language for worship. They further declared Thamizh, as Ghost language (Paisacha Bhasha), since it was devoid of Bhakthi (devotion) in it.

In 11th Century A.D., Ramanuja Muni took control of the temple with the support of Kooresan, Chieftain of Kooranadu, a commune, near Kanchipuram. (Kooresan bequeathed his throne and followed Ramanuja and assisted in all his efforts. Kooresan was a Mudali, one of the three sects, viz., Kone, Velh and Mudali, of Pallavas).

Ramanuja sent away the Konka priests and brought back the original Thamizh priests and introduced reciting Azhwar's Naalaayiram psalms (Tamizh) in the Temple as the prime ritual in the worship of Lord Arangan. But he failed to bring back Vall(h)uvars, to continue the astronomical pursuits.

CHAPTER 2

Mayans:

About 5,100 Years ago, when Catastrophe rocked the World, Mayans moved to safer places. Mayans, living in the Eastern part of 'Kandava vana, settled down in the forest lands situated in the east of Bay of Bengal. These places are now known as Myanmar, Thailand and further to Cambodia and Laos, and settled down.

Myanmar is a Phonetic variant of "Mayanmar"—Thamizh (Tamil), meaning, "Mayan Clan"..

On the west, they moved into what is known today as Tamil Nadu, and to the island, now known as Sri Lanka.

Brief history of the island, Sri lanka: Prior to 5,100 years, it was part of South India, linked by shallow landscape. Pebbles and gravels were spread over it. On the west of this landscape was a Range of Hills, mentioned as 'Gandhamathana Parvatha, in Valmiki Ramayana. The word 'Gandha' refers to Sandalwood, i.e., sandalwood trees were abundant on these hills, In addttion to this, various herbal trees and plants were also grown in that area. **This area was denoted as Kumarik kandam in Thamizh History.** A River, called 'Pahruli Aaru', was flowing from Southern hills towards west/southwest, along Gandhamathana Parvatha, turned left, passed through the valley (between Mandapam and Pamban, the land mark of the present times) again turned southwardly and merged with Indian Ocean. Pahru is the short form of the word,'Pahrukkaik kal', meaning, 'Small gravels/pebbles'. Thereby, the name of the river implies that, 'the river with gravels and pebbles spread over its bed'.

During the Catastrophe huge waves pushed the sand from the Eastern sea shores of the Bay of Bengal and dumped over the shallow land. Since the sea level also raised by about 30 meters, Sea indundated the land. Thus an island was carved out, which is called today as Sri Lanka.

In earlier days it was called **"Sinkala Theevu"**. (Sinkala Island). During Lord Buddha's period, i.e., 6/5th B.C., it was referred to as Sinhala Dweepa. Dweepa in Pali Language meant Theevu, i.e., Island. Sinhala is the Phonetic Variant of Thamizh word, Sinkam. The migrated Mayans were called, 'Sinkalavar', i.e., 'Sinhalese', as they are known today.

When Lord Buddha left Mortal World in 487 B.C., his Mortal remains were kept in State, by the Malla Kings, for ten days. During this period, followers of Buddha from Middle East, China, far East and Sinhala Dweepa, arrived there and paid their last respects. On the eleventh day, Malla Kings consigned his Mortal Remains to Flames. Thereafter, followers collected the ashes and returned to their countries. One tooth was left in tact, which Sinhalese took in a Golden casket and returned to their Country. Bikku Ananda Thera, was always with Lord Buddha, learnt all that were preached by the Lord. The Lord himself told him once that, that he thought that the "Buddha Sanga', instituted by self, would last for 2,500 years, and seeing the later developments, he feared that it might not last even for 500 Years. Remembering the Lord's words, Bikku Ananda Thera also left along with Sinhalese to Sinhala Dweepa. There the Golden Casket was interned at Kandy, Buddha's statue in Reclining Posture was installed, and Buddha Vihara was also built. This has become the seat of Theravada Buddha Sangam" preaching, righteously, the teachings of Lord Buddha.

This Theravada Buddhism is followed by Sinhalese, Myanmar (Mayanmnar) Buddhists, people of Laos, Cambodia and Thailand. The teachings of Buddhism were in Colloquial Pali. Influenced by this language, the languages spoken by the people of the abovementioned countries were blended with Pali, and new languages evolved.

During this period, i.e., 2,200 years ago, people of Tamil Nadu, (Tamilians as is commonly known) were already practicing Sakhya philosophy, and were secular, cherished and practiced their own Code, popularly known as "Kural". and did not follow any Ideological Religion. Buddha was venerated by them as one of the great seers, but kept their identity in tact.

People of Tamil Nadu, Buddhists of Sri Lanka (Sinhala), Myanmar, Laos, Cambodia and Thailand follow Vall(h)uvam- Samvathsaram Calendar, New Year commencing from Chithirai 1, which falls on April 14/15 of Gregorian Calendar.

Cutting short, let us take up the Mayan's Treatise, commencing with how they computed Time.

Map of Eastern Hemisphere.

1) The shallow landscape of Southern tip of India and surrounding Sri Lanka was called Kumari kantam. The shallow landscape submerged, carving out Sri Lanka as an Island.

2) The rock form in the middle of Bay of Bengal, extending down south upto Antartica, denoted Kandava vana. It can also been seen that Andaman &Nicobar, branching out like deer-horn, and the shallow landscape along Indonesian islands, Southern part, west of Australia, that were submerged during the catastrophe, which rocked the world, about 5,100 years ago.

Map showing sunken areas around Anndamans, South of Bengal, East of Myanmar Thailand &Malaysia shores and around Indonesian islands. Madura Island can be seen at North east of Jawa.

Kankeyan Island, which formed part of submerged Madura.

A view of the pit-like formation in the Sea Shore of Kankeyan Island. This is where experts dive in and collect pearl-oysters. This has similarity to Thoothukudi in South Tamil Nadu, where too Pearl Experts dive in and collect Pearl-Oysters.

Another scenario of Bull Race. OnJanuary 15th, next day to Pongal is celebrated as Mattu Pongal (cattle day) in Tamil Nadu, during which they conduct Bullock Cart Race. In addition to it, in Tamil Nadu they even perform "Taming the Bull", in which youths exhibit their valour.

Cows are decorated and taken in procession in Madura Island. On Cattle Day, inTamil Nadu too, Cows are decored and taken out. They are also fed sweet rice.

CHAPTER 3

Vall(vh)uvam – Astronomy

Kaalam (Time)

Mayan (m - as consonant, indicates mass/matter. Aya –Function based on mass as the prime one. 'n' - case ending. As such the nomenclature refers to those, who took mass/matter as the Basis of knowledge, studied and analysed their functions, their utility and process, in pursuit of knowledge, viz., Physical and Chemical fields, which indicates that they were Scientists and Technocrats.

One of the Aya Kalais of Mayans is 'Vall(h)uvam', i.e., Astronomy, in which, Kaalam (Time) plays a vital Role. They marked a Centre on Visuvathanam (equator) as the Point of Day-break for calculating time and date. This centre was at 90 degrees Meridian – east. From there, they went northwards, passing Imaya kootam(known today as Himalayas), Paarkadal – milky sea, (Arctic Ocean), Pani paarai kadal (sea of icebergs – Hudson Bay), and through a very wide landscape, narrowing by one-tenth, and reached a place, where they made a Mark of Naal(h)Varai-Date Line, i.e., one side Day and the other night. (Naal(h) – date and varai –line)

This is now revealed by the Western Archeologists/ Astronomers that this mark is in Mexico at 90 degrees Meridian-west. They have also made a mention of Mayans. In Srimad Bhagavatham, the Mayan is referred to as "Paramacharya Mayan", i.e., Eminent Professor Mayan.

Vall(h)uvam: [Vall(h)- Basis of prosperity; uvam-pleasing/agreeable.] - Astronomy. Based on the findings, they compiled the Almanac termed, "Kaala thiru kanitham", i.e., Mathematics of Time. This was also twisted after 2nd Century A.D. as Thiru kanitha Panchankam (removing Kaalam and suffixing a new found word Panchanka –i.e., of five limbs, viz., Time, Date, Star, month, and Year.)

Let us now analyse as to how they computed Kaalam – Time.

Core of Nature is termed as Karu, the stage when even the perennial natural waves were not manifested, and is termed as Thin(h) – Potential Energy. It was also explained as Thiruttham, meaning 'Absolute'.

Thin(h) takes the Prime stage for Creation, termed as An(H). [As 'A' is the prime alphabet, it is termed to denote as Prime state of Thin(h)]

An(h)u -The matter in which action commences, being induced by An(h). (An(h) - Prime one; U- undhu –Induce)

An(h)am – An(h) positions itself in An(h)u, i.e., as Kaala kattam- time frame, i.e., period. Kaalam is only a measurement, commencing when work starts and ceases when work ends.

As action commences from An(h)u-Atom, Kaalam also is computed from Atom, as Parama An(h)u Kaalam –Time based on Basic Atom.

1. **Parama An(h)u Kaalam** (Time based on Basic Atom. – Microcosmic Time.

Thiruvati: (Thiru –blemish less/unvarying; Ati –Step), i.e, the unvarying basic step of kaalam – Time.

Appu Vaayu (Hydrogen) is the Basic Atom, in which, one Electron (Virinchi in Thamizh), orbits in its only shell (Thamizh terms: Orbiting –parivalam; orbit shell – parivattom; each shell an An(h)am, i.e., period). As a basic atom, atomic weight commences as 'one'. Appu is unstable, as one electron cannot retain itself alone in the orbit. These Basic atoms link themselves in two "Triangular forms" in juxta position, such that, the six tips of the two triangles are positioned in a circle. [This form is mentioned as Charavan(h)u]. It is also stated, that they saw this form thus: - Fingers of two palms are positioned, opposite to each other, forming aperture between Centre and ring fingers, by entwining the fingers closely. If looked at sun at midday through this aperture, one can find six glowing tiny lobes as the (tips) points of these triangular shapes. The atom on one tip moves to link with one at the second tip, while the one at the second tip move to the third tip and so on, such that these movements are on a circle, and by this activity Parama An(h)u Kaalam commences.

Thus, the time taken by one Parama An(h)u- Basic Atom to reach the other is termed, "One Thiruvati". This term will hereafter be denoted as 'T".

5 T's = One Ilavam (step of process).

100 Ilavams (500 T's) = one Ilakku (Target).

7 Ilakku's (3,500 T's) = 1 Kantam (Section).

10 Kantams (35,000T's) = One Samam (Total)

25 samams (875,000T's) = One Kanam

Kanam – Kan(h) –eye. Am- amaithal – register. Thus, the time taken for any Image looked at, to register in eye.

Ten kanams – 8,750,000 T's - <u>one Naati</u>. Naati - Equivalent to one standard Pulse. (Naati – pulse)

Though pulses vary from one to the other depending on physical constitutions, professions, etc., i.e., 54 to 72 a Minute, here, for time calculation it is taken as 60 pulses a minute as Standard unit. Hence Naati is equivalent to one second. From Naati, Nara kaalam commences.

2. **Nara kalam (Human Time)**.

Nara –Human. Na- subservience; ra- activities. Thus, the one that is subservient in its (his) activities, by framing codes of life. This word is used as a term in psychological studies, and in calculation of Time.

24 Naatis – One Vinaati.

6 vinatis – one Naazhikai

2-1/2 Naazhikai's – on Orai. Hora is the phonetic variant, and from that, Hour.

2 Orais – One Chaamam.

6 Chaamams form the day time, and 6 Chaamams make the night time. Thus, 12 Chaamams make a Day (date).

Iraasi – Ira – Natural activity; and rasa – concentrate. Hence, Iraasam – Concentrate as natural activity, referring to the Beam of Sunlight. (m – Case ending).

Function of the beam of Sunlight is termed as "Iraasi".

Paanu:-Just as Visuvathanam for earth, Mayans marked the equator for Sun also, and termed it as Paanu.

This term is of three syllables – pa + an +u. Pa – patruthal, i.e., to hold; An- (core word) - Prime concept of control- here it denotes, 'Prime control, and, U- undhu, i.e., induce. Thus, this terms means, "To hold as the Prime control and induce".

The beam of Sunlight is formed with Paanu as the Prime control, and falls on earth, and Iraasi caculations are based on this aspect.

"A Spur Gear, meshed with an Involute Gear (inwardly), while rotating anti-clockwise, traverses clockwise along the Involute Gear. Similarly, when the Earth, while rotating anti clockwise on its own axis, traverses around Sun clockwise".. (Thamizh terms: Gear – Pal chakkaram; Involute Gear – Ull(h) amaintha pal Chakkaram. Pal-tooth.). This is a metaphorical explanation.

By this method Iraasam (Beam of Sunlight) functions. Function of Iraasam is termed as 'Iraasi'.

Every Month is termed as a Iraasi in the Time table, which is denoted as Iraasi Kattam, with twelve blocks.

In the same table, each Block is also marked as a Chaamam (two Orais-hours) and thus, the twelve blocks show the twelve Chaamams of a Day.

Parivaccharam:- The Trajectory of the Earth around Sun is termed, "Parivattom", and the earth's circumambulation is termed, 'Parivaccharam".

The Earth's revolving around its own axial control is termed, "Idavaccharam".

Iraasi varai: - The Earth's inclination as 22-1/2 thithis (degrees) was arrived at by Mayan with reference to the stars, 1) Thiruva (Pole star), 2), Apichith and 3) Arunthathi.

When observed from Vata Munai (North Pole)of the Earth, one could see Thiruvan (Pole Star) right above the head, Arunthathi star at half the right angle (45 thithis –degrees), and Apichith Star at bisecting angle between Thiruvan and Arunthathi (22-1/2 thithis). Likewise when observed from Visuvathanam (Equator), while Thiruvan was observed horizontally in the north. Apichith was observed in the same direction at 77-1/2 thithis), and Arunthathi was observed at 45 thithis in the same direction.

Iraasi varai Latitudes): With Visuvathanam as Centre, they marked 90 lines on the Northern hemisphere, and 90 lines on the Southern Hemisphere (total 180 thithis).

Based on the Iraasi (Beam of Sunlight) falling on these lines, they computed the Month and the Year.

Puvi: [pu – purithal, i.e., to perform) vi- virivu, i.e., vast & expansive. Viz., The Earth that performs expansively.

While it revolves on its own axis, it circumambulates around the Sun on Clockwise direction.

Iravi: - (Ira –Natural activity vi- vast/expansive) Sunlight from the day break to sunset

Kataka Iraasi:- While the Earth traverses, the last Iraasi Varai(latitude), where the beam of Sunlight, with Paanu. (Sun's Equator) as the centre, falls on the Northern Hemisphere, i.e., Line of Cancer. (Kata – katathal - passing, katai – last point). Hence Kataka varai, means, the last latitude at which the beam of Sunlight falls straight in the north.

Parivattom, the trajectory of the earth, is elongated and also widens, the Sunlight, Iraasi, falls on earth far beyond the angle of inclination, i.e., Kataka Iraasi at 23-1/4 thithis (degrees).

Makara Iraasi- The latitude passing through Makara Theevu, (Australian Island), which refers to "The line of Capricorn". This is the last latitude on which the Beam of Sunlight with Paanu as Centre, falls on the Southern Hemisphere, which is at 22-1/2 thithis (degrees)-same as the inclination of earth..

[Makara Theevu is what is known today as Australia. Makara refers to very huge Crocodiles of ancient times. They were so huge that they grasped and pulled the elephants as prey, and ate them, with the result; the whole Elephant species in the island was annihilated. This part of history of evolution is told in the form of folklore, Gajendra Moksha, Gajendra- Elephant species, Moksha – liberation. Even today, the natives in this continent treat Crocodiles as the holy ones - considered to be the first of the reptile species during the evolution of life system.]

Thisai varai: Itavattam - Earth revolves on its own axis, covering 360 thithis (degrees) and this is termed Idavaccharam: Each thithi is marked and termed "Thisai Vari", i.e. Latitudinal lines. It is the one based on which directions, enabling to know the place/position, and relative time as well for each place, is marked.

Reference mark was made on Visuvathanam (Equator Kaandava vanam as Day Break. (at 90 degrees-East, Meridian).

Tamizh terms further to Iravi:

Iravu:– Night. Natural activity –Ira, is confined within the physic, while externally it sleeps.)

Irul(h): Darkness. Though natural activities go on, they cannot be seen without light.

Iraahu kaalam:- Period of Solar eclipse. Ira - Natural activity; Aahu – almost over (Opposite term to Aakku- to prepare).

Kethu kaalam:- Period of Lunar eclipse. [kethu – kaa +e+thu; kaa –kaalam-(Time), e- Iyarkai-natural, thu- thuyil-slumber), i.e., slumber naturally through a particular period of Time. The landscape around the Arctic ocean is called Kethu Maalai (kethu garland), as these places are immersed in Darkness caused by Earth's own shadow. throughout the day for almost six months, when beam of Sunlight traverses in the Southern Hemisphere during this period.

Likewise, when Earth's shadow falls on Moon on any Full Moon's Day, causing Lunar Eclipse, that period is termed "Kethu kaalam".

YEAR

The Earth traverses around the Sun covering 360 thithis (Degrees). One Cycle is termed a Year. It is divided into 12 parts of each 30 thithis (degrees). Each part is denoted as a Month.

During circumambulation by the Earth, Beam of Sunlight (Iraasi) traverses from Southern Hemisphere towards Northern Hemisphere. The day on which Visuvathaam (Equator) and Paanu (equator) of Sun are on the same plane, is the first day of the Year.

Even though the Earth's traverse is at uniform speed, the trajectory widens after the first day, and after the second month it converges towards Kataka Iraasi (Line of Cancer), to take round-about turn. Because of this phenomenon, it takes 31 days for covering 30 thithis (degrees) during the first month, 32 days to cover during the second month, and 31 days during the third month. After the round-about turn the Earth continues to circumambulate, it takes 31 days for the fourth month,(replica of third month), and 32 days for the 5th month (replica of the second month), and 30 days for the sixth month (as the trajectory converges, closer to the Sun).

While the earth continues its traverse, the trajectory, converges when the Visuvathanam comes on the same plane with Paanu. Thereafter, it takes 30 days a month for next three months, i.e., 7th to 9th month. After this, (Iraasi) Beam of Sunlight passes over (Makara Iraasi) the Line of Capricorn; the trajectory converges a bit and normalises again during the last three months, 30 days for the 10th month, 29 days for the 11th and 30 days for the 12th month.

Thus, for first 3 months:-31 +32+31 = 94 days.

For next 3 months: 31+32+30 = 93days

Total for the northern hemisphere…….. = 187 days.*

3rd quarter – 3 months=30+30+30 days=90 days.

4th quarter – 3months= 29+29+30 days=89 days.

Total for the southern Hemisphere… = 178days.

Thus, No. of days for the whole year = 365 days.

* Few Hours less, but day calculation is based on day-break.

Though the Earth takes 365 days for one cycle of circumambulation, The period has to be computed, taking into consideration-Idavaccharam, i.e., Earth's rotation on its own Axial control (day calculation).

When a particular place is facing Sun on Daybreak (Iravi) on any New Year Day, and, after the circumambulation cycle, on the first day of the second year, there is a time lag of that particular place to face Iravi (Day break). This time lag was also computed as 6 Orais (hours), 53 vinaatis and 4 naatis, which is equivalent to 6 Hours, 23 minutes and 40 seconds. [Note: this figure furnished pertains to the latest period of year]. 23 minutes and 4 seconds is rounded off as 24 minutes, i.e., One Naazhikai. Of this, 6 hours is computed as one day and added to the Year, i.e., 366 days once every four years, and this day is added to eleventh month (Maasi). The balance of 1 Naazhikai is shown in Kaala Thirukkanitham 'as Balance on the New Year Day. This is computed for every 60 years and added as one day to the 61st year. By the same procedure, one day was added to 2010 A.D.. Though this was accepted/computed by the western Scientists, status quo in the no. of days of that year was maintained, as it was found that any variation would lead to ramifications in various fields, especially in financial dealings, due to dependence on Computer operational techniques. But in Thamizh/Samvacchara year it was accounted, and thus the first day of New Year, coincided with April 15, instead of April 14, the usual Date.

The Year is termed as Samvacchara Aandu (Samvacchara Year), and it is computed with the following three time factors;-

1) Parivaccharam – Earth's circumambulation around Sun.
2) Idavaccharam - Earth's Rotation on its own axial control
3) Anuvaccharam – Moon's circumambulation around Earth, under Earth's Axial control. (An - Prime Control, i.e., Earth's Axis; U-undu i.e., induce).

The Almanac is termed, "Kaala Thiruk kanitham". [Twisted as 'Thirukanitha Panhankam after 2nd Century A.D. by the Cherars-migrants.].

CHAPTER 4

Manvanthiram – Earth's Age.

Manvanthiram: - M-mass, Earth; an- prime control; va-(vaham)-taking responsibility on its own; Thiram-capability; Thus the word implies, "Capability of Earth's Axial Control.

This is based on Nara (Human) Kaala kanitham (Standard Time computation). Let us analyze how the calculation of Earth's Age and Time were taken up.

Manvanthiram calculation commenced after the Earth passed out of Sun, and became a Planet, taking responsibility for the Nature's activities upon itself.

Even though the Earth circumambulates covering 360 thithis (degrees) for every cycle, by Idavatta calculation (Naal(h) - Day), it takes 365 days, thereby there is an increase of 5 days. Over the radial figure of 360 thithis (degrees).

This number of five days is figured out thus:.
24 naatis x 60 vinaatis x 60 naazhikais x5 days) i.e,
24 x 60 =1440 naatis = 1 Naazhikai.
60 Naazhikais =1 day i.e., 1440 x60 = 86,400 Naatis

[Also computed -1440 x 2 =2880 x30 = 86,400; This calculation pertains to day + night, i.e., Day-30 Naazhikai and night of 30 Naazhikais.].

Hence for 5 days = 86,400 Naatis x 5 = 432,000 Naatis,
Where Naati (second) is the Basic time.

As the Earth came out of Sun in spiraling mode, it slowly distanced away from Sun, thereby its distance from Sun increased. This distance is assessed on the basis of Kaalam (Time). By this principle, Mayans computed that, the Year, the period of circumambulation increases by One Naati (second) for every 20 years.

This One Naati is taken as the basic Unit of time, also taking every second as 20 years of the earth, Manvanthira Kaalam(time), is,

432,000 x 20 = 8,640,000 Years.

The Earth:

As the Earth was formed in Sun it was a globe of Kadir thukal's (Radio active particles), and was super hot because of Radiation, as it was part of Sun. While it was spiralling and drifting towards the outer periphery of Sun, as a mass, gases were attracted by the Earth engulfing it. Some of these gases were,

1) Appu Vaayu: (Hydrogen gas), 2) Itha Vaayu(Helium gas), 3) Nela Vaayu(Chlorine), 4) Thita Vaayu(Nitrogen), 5) Aalakalam (Fluorine), 6) Mukkan(h) Asu Vaayu (Trivalent Oxygen, i.e., Ozone).

When the Earth moved out of Sun, it was like a "huge fire ball", because of (Maa Perum Anal Thiran) Super Thermal Energy, and started circumambulating Sun on Parivattam (trajectory).

As the Parivattom was of spiral-form, It was enlarging, thereby the distance of the Earth increased. The various stages, **The Pookol(h)am** (Global Earth) underwent from its formation in the Core of Sun, as narrated by Mayans in Vall(h)uvam, are detailed as below:

1. **Ulaka Thotram**-Genesis of Earth:

Core of the Sun: Kaanal- Mareechi – m+ar+ee+chi: M-Mei -Mass); Ar-Prime concept of activity; ee –Eantru –Yeilded, chi –chiranthu uruthal – performing to a greater extent. This word thus imply that, the core of Sun takes the Prime stage for yielding the mass (the Earth), and also take prime stage of activity, such that it (mass – Earth) can perform to a great extent (or extensively). Kaanal: (K –basis of Work through time, action; +Anal (Anal thiran, Thermal Energy) Action of very high temperature due to super thermal Energy.

Kathir thuk(h)alkal (Radio Active particles) and vasus- Basic particles, collected as clouds and by the gravitational(Eerpu) and Centrifugal action (Mei chuzhal thanmai) formed Array of clouds (Meka kootangal), and started to circumambulate outside the Core, from left to right direction (Clockwise). As there was no mass in the core, Kaanal), the clouds entered it on the right side, (as water was poured into a large vessel from a pipe on one side, which slowly fills up), and swirled in the core from right to left, and gradually filled it up, thus forming the Puvi (The Earth). The earth took to rotation in the same direction while filling, Valam-Idam, -from right to left (Anti - clockwise).

As the core was saturated with formation of the Earth, more number of clouds collected as another Globe, and started to circumambulate outside the periphery of Kaanal - Core. This Globe was very fierce by the Radio activity, just as the Earth.

The Axial Control of the Sun was denoted as Vivasuvaan.

Vivasuvan – Vi+ Vasu+Va+An.: Vi - vithikkappatta- Established, vasu – Basic particle, va-vakham –Taking responsibility on its own, an- prime control (Thamizh core word). Prime control of the one established with Basic Particles, i.e., The Axial Control of the Sun.

The Axial Control is not a material formation. As the Global Mass formed later to the Earth, was circumambulating close to the Core, it naturally came under the axial control of the Earth as it was a huge Mass, greater than itself. As Vivasuvaan did not hold any mass for itself, and as the second mass too interacted with its axial control, the Earth was tilted by 22-1/2 thithis (degrees). Now the Earth's Axis was different from that of the Sun, and as it was rotating in a different position, the Earth, naturally, slipped out of the Core and started moving around, clockwise, close to it (core). As already narrated, the second mass started circumambulating the Earth, and became its satellite Planet, which was later called "the Moon".

As the Moon was formed outside the Core of Sun, it did not gain an Axis for itself, and moved stable. Therefore, it was termed 'Nila' (Thamizh nomenclature), meaning, 'stable'.

2. <u>Athiram</u> – Prime capability of activity. This nomenclature was later written as Atthiram. After the Earth came out of the Sun's Core, it passed through this Athira Stage, and it gained the responsibility as a planet.

3. <u>Ankirasam</u>: Anka +Irasam; Anka- limb or part; Irasam- Concentrate; At this stage the Radio active particles identified their own kindred, forming concentrates, resulting in the cloud formations turning to concentrated vapour (Irasam) form, and also formed as limb or Part of the Earth.

4. <u>Pulayam</u>:- Pul(ar))+yam. Pula – Pular: Dawn, yam – function. (As a word, it is written as Iyam-function). Density of the outer periphery of Sun, was very low, and was gaseous. Several Radio active Particles were in gaseous stage and less intensive. When Earth reached this stage, it collected the Gaseous Radio Active Particles as its own Atmosphere (Ozone was an exception, and it could not be turned Kathir (Radio Active)).

5. <u>Pularnthiym</u>:- pularnthu +Iyam. The stage in which the Earth was dawned, moved out of Sun's periphery, on its own, and then started functioning as a

separate entity. The Moon followed the Earth and started circumamblating it on its Trajectory- Anuvattom, under the Axial Control of the Earth.

6. <u>Ka</u>vi: - Ka+vi.- <u>Ka</u>dappadu <u>Vi</u>rivadaithal.. The underlined first alphabets of the words are combined to form this Word. Kadappadu – Various activities based on Time factor; Virivadaihal - Expansive and enlarge into different varieties, i.e., The Earth's activities commenced in various ways. The burning Globe of the earth started to cool down while it was moving away from the Sun.

During the course of time, the Earth reached a stage when the day time of the Earth came to an end, and the twilight evening time began. This was depicted that, pakal kaalam (day time) ended, and Rule of Iran(h)iya began.

[Iran(h)iya Aatchi– expanded as 'Iravu'(night) +An(h)a (period of time)+Iyam-function. Aatchee – Rule].

7. <u>Anthi</u> (Twilight Evening): - Kathir thukals, i.e., the Radio active particles, could not affect Mukkan(h) Asu (Trivalent Oxygen, i.e., Ozone) by radiation. Ozone grappled and oxidized these particles, thereby they slowly lost their rigour, and in due course they turned into kasam, i.e., residuary particles, and the Earth's atmosphere was clouded with these particles as dust. As the Sun's light could not reach the Earth, it became almost dark, and as the earth was glowing with very hot high density mass, it looked as though (Anthi) twilight evening spread over the Earth.

This stage was described as "Iran(h)iya Kaalam"(Period of night time), and also Iran(h)iya Kasipu Aatchi-Rule of Iran(h)iyam, because of the residuary particles).

[In Sanskrit versions, it is mentioned as the Rule of Hiranya kasipu, which is only phonetic variant of Thamizh terms. Moreover it looked as in night, is mentioned as Hiranyaksha, wherein Hiranya is a phonetic variant of Thamizh-Iranyam, and Aksha – look/sight]

In the course of Time, most of the kasams (residuary particles) turned Poothams (mass, blossomed in nature) i.e., Elements. Still some of the radio active particles of higher An(h)ams (Periods/shells) remained as Asurams (Oxidised Radio Active particles). It was mentioned that there were eight Asurams in the Earth.

As the earth continued to cool down (below 3,000 degrees Celsius as per CGS), Mahi (Graphite) and Kalnaar (Asbestos), making a compound, solidified and formed the crust termed, Mahi Thalam, i.e., Very hard and rigid Stratum, and a bad conductor of heat.

As the temperature still cooled, the metals and non metals, forming alloys/compounds, cooled at different ranges of temperatures, and according to the ranges, they all formed plates over plates. (as crusts), over the Mahi Thalam. At this stage glow of the Earth ceased and darkness fell on it, as the atmosphere was filled with massive Dust covering very high altitude. As the temperature lowered to a great extent, and at this stage, Appu vaayu (Hydrogen) teamed with (Iru Kan(h)Asu) bi-valent oxygen, burnt and Aapasu irasam, i.e., Water vapours formed in atmosphere. This was metaphorically described thus: "The Earth was immersed in ocean during the night." Finally, when the temperature fell below the boiling point of water, water vapour turned liquid. Then all the dust along with water fell on the Earth, with massive force, forming the two strata, Vithalam of various metals and non metals of higher specific Gravity (oppidai), and over which Athalam (Primary stratum) of mud and water formed.

Then the sky became clear, and as Sunlight fell on Earth, the second day dawned.

[The enlightened scholar, who invented this great truth, was decorated as, "Chithar Kaasiyapar", meaning, 'Enlightened, who achieved the great knowledge of Kasipu (residuary particles'. He was also praised that Kaasiyapar gave birth to the two, Iran(h)ya Kasipu, the elder, and Iran(h)yaksha, the younger, which only meant that they were his "brain children".].

The period up to Anthi, was termed as Manvanthira –day time, Anthi as Manvanthira night time, together forming Manvanthira day. This forms part of Earth's age.

This first day is termed "Aathi Varaaka Karpam" Aathi – Primary+vara-Taking responsibity to perform;+ aka-initiating activities, karpam- methodically over a period of time; Thus the nomenclature implies, "The period (Day) during which Earth took responsibility upon itself and initiated the primary activities."

The second Day dawned is termed "Poovaraaka Karpam". Poo-Blossomed; varaaka- Taking responsibility on its own to perform; Karpam-methodical over a period of time), i.e., The Earth 'blossomed', taking responsibity to perform methodically based on time factor

8. Rule of Kasipu: Nature's performance began to rule after the Residuary Particles formed the Earth's surface as Athalam(Prime Stratum), and also after the dawn, the schedules of time as Day and night commenced.

This period was very interesting. The sky was bright, and humid, temperature reduced phenomenally, and the earth was slushy and with lot of water, several places were also quagmires. Algae as the first form of life system spread all over the earth, and it looked beautiful as though covered with green carpet. Then Naan(h)al, a thin plant with its roots with rigid grip, belonging to Bamboo family, sprouted and spread out wildly.

9. A(h)kani: (Sanskrit word-Agni is a phonetic variant of Thamizh word): -a(h) k – Prime concept of Involvement; An - Prime concept of control, and e-enablement. Thus this word implies that, "Enablement of involvement under Prime control of Nature".

It manifests in three stages, viz., 1) Patruthal –Catching, 2) Padarthal –spreading, and Seeraadal-neutralising.

[Note -15 A(h)kanis are mentioned, mainly, 1) Sankara A(h)kni Rays emanating from Neutron, i.e., Gamma Ray; 2) Savitha thevam, i.e., Kariya Sivantha Alai, i.e., Infra Red Rays, 3) kathir veechu – Radiation from Radio Active Particles, 4) Erimalai kuzhambu, i.e., Lava 5) Kattu thee- forest fire, 6) Kaalavai thee -Fire in furnaces, etc, 6) Neruppu– controlled fire used in homes for cooking, lighting, etc. 7) kiratina a(h)kani- oxidation, 8) Amila A(h) kani – Acid, 9) Asava A(h)ani- Alkaline and alcoholic, (10) Kan(h)ai choodu - Temperature in various glands (several are added to the list as different fires, and are followed by Chittha (known commonly as Siddha) physicians. In addition, psychologically, Anger, Enmity, avarice, Intolerance out of jealousy, lust, etc., are also defined as A(h)kanis.]

Let us again continue from the stage of 'Kasipu'. The dried leaves of Naan(h) al dropped on the slush, rotted, from which Eri Vaaiyu (fire gas, i.e., Methane gas) spread into the atmosphere, contacted oxygen in the atmosphere and caught fire on its own. Water on the earth evaporated because of the rise in temperature, formed clouds and it rained in the evening hours as a regular feature.

While the evolution of life system commenced as, Viyarvayil Uyirthal- sprout from humidity – Algae, and then immovable plant, as grass and Naan(h) al, the second one as Plant, a thin and small variety of bamboos.

Then movable life system also evolved.. Termites, evolved from the rotten leaves, built termite-hills everywhere, by which the earth hardened, and water resistant, resulting in development of dry earth surfaces. Moreover, whenever rain-water entered these hills, the Termites grew wings on their own and flew out of the pits. From this, in due course, evolved the flying life system commencing from winged ones, viz., Bees and then honey bees which biologically belong to termite/ant family.

During this period, being the initial ones, there were no mountains/hills, rivers seas, lakes, etc.. However, there were, of course several Mole hills (Aathi Varaaka Kundru), formed as Sedimentation over the Plates, when the crusts formed. One such in Then Thiruvidam (South India) is what is now called,

"Thirumala Hills", also known as Venkatam, These hills are also declared holy ones as Aathi Varaaka Chethiram. (Chethiram – Matured and cherished capability of Nature).

(This Part is only concerned with Earth's Age i.e., Manvanthiram. Evolution of Nature and Evolution of Life System, is dealt with separately in later part of this book, under the title, "Creation from core of Nature")

10) <u>Naaratha Stage</u>:- Na- non existence of matter and not even natural perennial waves(nothingness, i.e., Core) +nara- Human, who is subservient and acts, +tha- knowledge conceived within oneself. Thus the word implies, "The knowledge conceived, covering from the Nature's Core to the Human.

As is clear from the nomenclature itself, subsequent evolution of Nature and followed by evolution of Life System also followed the Initial period.

Now let us continue the analysis on the age of the Earth (Page 34) as Manvanthiram.

Manvanthiram as a full day was computed as 8,640,000 Years. The evolution was only Part by Part, as day and night, Manvanthira kaalam is also is taken accordingly as, 4,320,000 Human years, (hereafter to be stated as year only).

Dividing 360 thithis-degrees by 5 days (the difference between thithis and number of days taken for circumambulation), we get 72, Which is taken as the number of manvanthirams for the Aadhi Varaaka day(time), and 72 Manvanthirams for the night of Aadivaraaka karpam. Thus,

First day of Aadi Varaaka Karpam:

Day time – 72 x 4,320,000 = 311,040,000 Years.

Night time - 72 x 4,320,000 = 311,040,000 Years.

First day of Aadi Varaka Karpam, as Earth's Age is:-

311,040,000 + 311,040,000 = 622,080,000 Years.

At present we are living in 28th Manvanthiram of Poovaraaka Karpam.

For the past 27 Manvanthirams =27 x 4,320,000 x27 equals: 116,640,000 years.

When the Earth came out the Sun's atmosphere, it was a huge mass, several times larger than at present, It was assessed by Mayans that, initially the Earth took 120 days as the year to traverse around Sun. They divided this by 5 and the quotient arrived at as 24 Manvanthirams. This, they accounted as the period the Earth took. from the Core of the Sun till it traversed out of Sun's atmosphere to Pularnthiyam stage(Dawn of Earth as Planet).

Thus time taken from the Core of the Sun to Pularnthiyam, i.e., release from Sun, is, 4,320,000 x 24 = 103,680,000 Years.(Taking as daytime) Thus, Earth's Age is,

Up to release from Sun - 103,680,000 years
Aathi Varaaka karpam((1st day) - 622,080,000 years
Poovaraaka Karpam(2nd 27M*)- 116,640,000 years

Total - 842,400,000 years.

This can be compared with the present scientific calculations.

CHAPTER 5

Para Kaalam -Macro Cosmic Time

Param - Macrocosm; Kaalam-Time.i.e., Macrocosmic time.

The distances in the vast Space cannot be assessed by whatever measuring Units followed by us in our routine life. Time and distance is the definition, and based on this time is taken up for this assessment of distances in space, Para Kaalam is devised as the measuring unit.

Para kaalam: It is mentioned that, Kaarunikan takes one Naati (second) to travel from Moon to the Earth.

Kaarunikan – The one, who can be seen as Minnal-lightning. The first syllable, "Min" is elaborated as Minsaaram, i.e., Electricity. Further it is stated that, he takes responsibility for various activities of the life system and physical activities in all living beings. This refers to the Static Electricity generated in the Glands and also in the movements of muscles. Kaarunika is also mentioned as the one, who has the form of Thevan, i.e., Perennial waves, mainly electronic waves.

By the statement in first paragraph, it denotes the speed of Waves, for a second.

The distance of Moon from earth on New Moon Day, normally, is 300,000 Kilo Meters. Its trajectory, Anuvattom, is not uniform as that of the Earth (Parivattom), and there are occasions when moon comes closer to the

Earth, i.e., up to 200,000 K.Ms. also. But for Uniformity of time, it is taken as 300,000 KMs.

Hence, Parakala Vehkam (speed) is measured at 300,000 KM.s a Second.

Parakaala Aandu (Para kaala Year) is the distance covered at 3,00,000 KMs./second in a year for 360 days (The standard year based on 360 thithis(degree) days a cycle of year.

It can be seen that Para Kaala Aandu is the same as "Light Year calculation followed by Western Scientists.

Para Kaala naal(h) – Para kaala day time – 1,000 Manvanthirams, i.e., 1,000 x 4,320,000 = 432, 000,000

.   years.

Para kaala night – 1,000 x432,000,000 = 432,000,000

Years. Total for a day – 864,000,000 years.

One para kaala year =864,000,000 x 360=

3,110,400,000,000 Years.

[Three Trillion One hundred and ten Billion and four hundred Million Years.]

This is the distance to the outer periphery of the Sana Ulakam, i.e., the Universe, in which the Galaxy of the Stellar constellations are created and are revolving around in their own trajectories without colliding with each other, and at the same drifting towards the edge of Sana Ulakam, the outer periphery of the Universe.

To reach this edge, it takes One Parakaala Aandu, for any matter, which includes stars also, by traveling at the speed of 300,000 KMs a second, for 3 Trillion, one hundred and ten Billion and four hundred Million Years.

The Universe is surrounded by Visuva Thevams (Cosmic Waves), i.e., Thapa Ulakam -the one that holds the Sana Ulakam. When the Matter enters this world, they are taken over and transformed into Waves of their own kind, and the matter ceases to exist.

As Cosmic Waves also travel perennially, they are also bound by Parakaala Aandu. Even while traveling, they too are expected to reach the outer periphery of Thapa Ulakam. This also is assumed to be one thousand Parakaala Aandu, and including this, a total number of years is 3 Zillion, One hindred and ten Trillion and three billion years.)

This Thapa Ulakam is surrounded by Vaikuntam, defined as Azhi, which means fence and also defined in true sense as below:

Azh –Karu – Core of Nature. Defined as Manivann(h)an- characteristic of a Pure Diamond, which cannot be contacted or spread within it, when the light waves pass through. Similarly Perennial Waves or any matter cannot touch or feel it. It is defined as "THIN(H)", the one that rules over the Strength, i.e., Potential Energy, and also as "Absolute", which is the Core is the source of Creation, primarily in Wave form.

Azh – The one, that does not have any dimensional features of matter, but is the prime one for creation of Waves and thereafter the matter, which possesses dimensions. To cut short, the definition of "Black Hole" by present day Scientists defines this.

Vaikuntam is the Black Hole surrounding the Thapa Ulakam, i.e., Cosmic World. It is the one termed as Azhi, that is, fence for all Waves and Matter, and as such the fence of Time also.

Therefore, considering the Cosmic Waves along the transformed matter into waves, drifting towards the periphery, it takes thousand years. Therefore the Parakaala distance as time is,

$$3,110,400,000,000 \times 1000 = 3,110,400,000,000,000 \text{ Years,}$$

i.e., Three Zillion one hundred and ten Trillion, and four

hundred Billion Years., After this period of time the Cosmic Waves reach Thapa Ulaka periphery.

When they try to enter Azhi, the Vaikuntam, the Waves ceases, looses their forms. With cessation of their activities they become part of the Eternity.

As activities ceases, Time also ceases to Exist.

CHAPTER 6

Earth and Time, and Samvaccharam Year.

To calculate time for each day, they marked the following four stages, depending on the position of Sun during daytime and stellar complexes at night.

1) Kaandava puri: When it dawns at the Eastern horizon, the Sky above is denoted as Kaandava Puri. (The senses awake and activities begin).

2) Maeravi While the Earth rotates from Right to left, the sky above is denoted as Maeravi(Sun above the head): Maa- vast, expansive;+Iravi-sunlight, i.e., Sunlight spreads expansively on left and right of this position, i.e., Noon time

3) Varuna Puri: When Sun is at the western horizon, the sky above is denoted a Varuna Puri. Varuna- Ionisation; Here it refers to activities of senses, devoid of professional activities, i.e., taking rest, indulging in games, music, etc.,

4) Yamapuri: Sky above at Midnight. Yama-function of life system. Even though the living beings sleep, various functions of the life system of the physic continue to function.

These four stages were initially denoted based on the Time-line marked in Kaandava Vanam (90 degrees, Meridian East) and later, these positions were denoted for each place, based on Thisai Varai (latitude).

CHAPTER 7

Aandu: (Year)

The day, on which Visuvathanam (Equator) of the Earth and Paanu (Equator) of the Sun come on the same Plane, is the first day of the Year.

Sankaraman(h)am and Sankaraanthi: (Equinoxes)

Sankaraman(h)am: Sankam – Association with a Purpose; An(h)am – Period. Thus, Sankaraman(h)am implies, "the period of Association with a purpose. Here it denotes the Period in which Visuvathanam and Paanu come on the same plane.

Sankaraanthi: Sankaram – already explained; Anthi –end/over; Thus, Sankaraman(h)am is over.

There are four Sankaraman(h)ams and subsequent Sankaraanthis, during the course of the Earth circumambulating the Sun., which are as below:

1) Ma(y)ta Sankaraman(h)am and subsequent Ma(y)ta Sankaraanthi: The time when Visuvathanam(Earth's) and Paanu(Sun's) come on the same plane when the Iraasi (Beam of Sunlight), while the Beam of Sunlight(Iraasi) traverses in Northern Hemisphere.

This Sankaraanthi is the first day of the year, viz. 1st day of the first month – Chithirai. (April 14)

2) Kataka Sankaraman(h)am and Sankaraanthi: Kataka (Iraasi) – In Thamizh- Kadatthalin kadainilai, i.e., the last stage up to which Iraasi passes in Northern hemisphere –i.e., Kataka Iraasi - Line of Cancer; Kataka Sankaraman(h)am - the period at which the Beam of sunlight reaches the Line of Cancer. Kataka Sankaraanthi –Sankaraman(h)am is over and Earth continues to traverse.

This Sankaraanthi is the first day of the fourth month- Aati.

3) Thula Sankaraman(h)am and Thula Sankaraanthi:
Thula- weighing scale. Here Iraasi is equipoised on both the hemispheres. The period during which Visuvathanam(Earth's) and Paanu(Sun's) come on same plane, when iraasi passes from the Northern to Southern Hemisphere.

This Thula Sankaraanthi is the first Day of the 7th Month- Aippasi.

4) Makara Sankaraman(h)am and Makara Sankaraanthi:
Makara denotes Makara Theevu, i.e., Australia. Makara Iraasi – Line of Capricorn. The period during which Iraasi reaches the Makara Varai-Line of Capricorn, and Makara Sankaraanthi, indicates the time at which Sankaraman(h)am was over, as the earth continues to traverse.

This Makara Sankaraathi is the first day of the 10th Month – Thai.

On the first day of the fourth month-Aadi Iraasi (the beam of Sunlight) commences to pass towards the Southern hemisphere. Similarly, on the first day of 10th month-Thai, Iraasi commences to pass toward Northern Hemisphere. Therefore, these two Sankaraanthis are celebrated as serene/holy celestial festivals, by those following Samvacchara kaala Thiruk kanitham (Almanac/ Calender).

Paruvam (Season). Period, during which, the natural variations are widely prevalent. These paruvams are computed for predictions, mainly taking agricultural operations into considerations.

[Note: - Due to indiscriminate denudation of forests, mining and population explosion have led to. the Natural predictions unreliable.]

1) Il(h)avaynil: Il(h)a – junior. Here it means first one. Va(y)nil-Summer. Thus, the word, Ilhavaynil indicates 'the first summer'. The first two months of the year, viz., Chithirai (April 14 to May 14) and Vaikaasi (May 15-June 15).

Kathiri: This is an important zodiacal event. Kathiravan indicates the Sun. Kathiri means, the function of Sun, i.e., the Sun's Light widely spreads towards the landscape from Kumari (Kanyakumari) Munai (cape) and Kataka Iraasi, and starts spreading towards the Landscapes beyond the Kataka Iraasi. From the 5th Iraasi Varai (5th Latitude), Sun's activity commences directly over the landscapes, especially Thiruvidam (India). It takes 20 days (4 days for each Iraasi Varai- Latitude, from the first day of Chithirai (April, 14) and Kathiri (Direct activity of Sun) begins on 20th Chithirai (May 3rd). Temperature is very high during this period, which lasts for about 14 days. After this, the (Kodai Kaatru) South West wind sets in and temperature starts falling.

2) Kodai Paruvam: Kuda thisai – West, and Kodai – South West. This refers to South West Monsoon. 3rd and 4th Month, i.e., Aani and Aadi months, commencing from June 15/16th. Though Monsoon commences on June 5th, it becomes vigorous, resulting in copious rainfall on the Western Ghats, and floods in the East-flowing Rivers, which is conducive to Agricultural operations.

3) Muthu Vaynil: Known as Second Summer, when iraai traverses towards Thula Iraasi. - This paruvam falls during the 5th and 6th months, viz., Aavani (August16-17th) and Purattaasi (September-16th). As there would be copious water flowing and the fields would be green with crops, temperature would be high but tolerable.

4) Kaar Paruvam: Kaar- Dark clouds resulting in incessant rains. This Paruvam falls during 7th and 8h months, viz., Aippasi (October 15/16th) and Kaarthikai (November 15th). Vaadai (vadakku-North and Vaadai-North-East) The North-East Mansoon brings heavy and incessant rains in Eastern coastal areas and hinterlands. Second Agricultural operation commences.

5) Mun Pani kaalam: Mun – prior; Pani-fog; The fog season. Rain ceases. This paruvam falls during 9th and 10th Months, Margazhi (December, 16th) and Thai (January 14th). As Iraasi traverses towards Makara Iraasi (Line of Capricorn), temperature falls down very low in eastern, hinterland and hillsides, due to rise in level of water table in the earth, snow fall commences on hills and fog spreads on platues and plains early evening/nights during these two months.

6) Pin Pani kaalam: Pin – Later (part) - the period later to Snowfall/fog. This covers 11th and 12th months, Maasi (February 14 /15th), and Panguni (March 13th).

On Aadi 1st,(July 17th), the beam of Sun light commences its Traverse towards Southern Hemisphere, and on 1st Thai (January 14th) the beam of sun light commences its traverse towards Northern Hemisphere. These two days are considered as Zodiacal feats of importance, and agriculture-related festivals ae held.

In Places around and North of Kataka Iraasi (Line of cancer), there are only three main Paruvams (Seasons), viz.,

1) Va(y)nil Paruvam (Summer), (12th Month, Panguni 1st to 3rd Month, Aani, 31st).

2) Kaar Paruvam(Rainy Season), 4th month, Aadi 1st to 7th Month, Aippasi 30th), and,

3) Kulhir Paruvam(Winter), (8th Month, Kaarthikai 1st, to 11th Month, Maasi 29/3th).

Moreover, (i) 1st of Pankuni (March 13th/14th), (ii) Aadi 1st (July 16th/17th), and (iii)Kaarthikai 1st (November 15th), are denoted as three Kumbams (Conical crest). These days are celebrated as festivals (Kumbh Mela) in Northern India.

CHAPTER 8

Planets born out of the Grand Sir, Sun, as per Vallhuvam

English version of one of the "Pallandu psalms" rendered by Peria Azhvaar of Thamizh - Kadai Chanka Period (B.C.500-250), King of Seervilliputthur (now called Srivilliputthur), is as below:

"The one who yielded life to us, the one yielded life to him, the one yielded life to him, the one yielded life to him, his father, grand father and great Grand father, beginning from the seventh step, we are performing our activities under "His control". The purport:

> The one yielded life to us– Planet Earth; (2) The one who yielded life to him – Planet Mars, on which life system ceased, and transcended to earth, (3) The one who yielded life to him – Planet Mercury, where life system ceased and transcended to Mars, (4) The one who yielded life to him – Planet Saturn, and

His father, Grand father and Great grand father, three planets formed in Sun's Core, prior to Saturn, but far away beyond the Axial control of the Sun.

From the above, we can see that ours is the seventh Planet borne out of Sun (mentioned as seventh step).

Note: As a finale in Mars, all were burnt to ashes, i.e., as strongly bonded carbonates nitro compounds, resulting in non availability of Organic ingredients, mainly Hydrogen, Oxygen, nitrogen, and Carbon. It is mentioned as (Erintha Sambal-Kuraipaadu) difficiency due to burnt ashes in that Planet, leading to cessation of life there.

(Note: In Sanskrit, it is mentioned as Ankaraka Dosham, wherein, Ankarakam-burnt ash, dosham-difficiency. This is exploited by Astrologers, mentioning Ankarakan, as the Planet and also the God of that Planet, and State that he causes wars, troubles in Societies/families. Though well educated, many people do not think on their own, bewildered as they are, give credence to such borrowed predictions.).

Even though it is the seventh Planet, let us commence with the facts on Earth, as furnished in Val(h)uvam.

Planet Earth:

This planet is also referred to as "Pankthi", i.e., Shift, implying that the present of Life system commenced and continues on our Planet after the shift in mars was over.

The constitution of this Planet is detailed as seven Strata as below:

1) Athalam: Prime Stratum (Thalam – stratum)- The surface, water table and depth to the extent the roots of Plants can go down, sea, and the atmosphere.

2) Vithalam: vi- first syllable of virivu, elaborate/spread out; thalam-stratum. The stratum below Athalam, spread out elaborately, containing metals (Ulokam) and non metals (alokam).

Alokam (Nonmetals) – kari - carbon, chilai - silicon, kanthakam - Sulphur, Oattappam- Phosphorous, kalnaar (Asbestos).

Ulokam(metals): Kambu(Calcium), Indu(Potassium), kambachhootam (Aluminium), Aiyan*(Iron); Eeiyam (lead), kalaayam(Tin), Thutthanaagam (Zinc), Chempu, (copper), Pon (Gold), Vell(h)i (Silver), Thananchayam (chromium), Paatharasam (Mercury), etc..

Gases in compounds with the above, and in atmosphere, which too forms part of Athalam: Asu - Oxygen, Appu-Hydrogen, Nela - Chlorine, Thida - Nitrogen, Aalahalam-Fluorine (With Kambu-Calcium), Itha-Helium(Only in vaanam - atmosphere).

Aiyan-Iron is always available with carbon being bonded to it, and as such is referred as irumpu, indicating mild steel.

Further, it is stated in the history of Evolution that in a catastrophe (deluge) during 25th Manvanthiram of Poovaraha Karpam (Present one), plates dashed agaist one another. Rocks that were cracked from Plates in the impacts and the earth were squeezed, and raised along with soil above <u>as mountains and hills</u>. Dense Forests were turned over and buried in deep pits occurred during such impacts. The crushed juices of the plants remain as lakes, deep under the Earth. Further, Lava of molten metal/non metals, are flowing like rivers, along the serpentine cracked junctions of Plates.

3) <u>Suva thalam</u>: su- suzhal- rotation; va-vaham- respon- sibity; thalam- stratum Thus, The Stratum in which para magnet is induced. This stratum is formed with the combination of Aiyan (Iron), Velhir Ulokam(nickel), kambachootam (Aluminium) and Chilai (silicon).

Moreover, It was also stated, that magnetic lines formed in its northern Poles rose like a Bamboo grove, above the Northern Pole of the Earth, high in the sky, spreads out all around, and reached the Southern Pole, like a Bamboo Grove.

This Magnetic field high above the sky, was denoted as 'Suvaanam' suva(of Suva thalam) +vanam-Grove) This is stated to be the limit of Earth's Gravitation (Thamizh – Eerpu).

This invention by the Mayans dates even before 7,500 years, the Year in which the first Thmizh Chankam (Literary Asociation) was instituted.

This Great truth can be verified and corroborated with "Van Der Vaal's Belt, invented during the early part of 20th Century A.D., by the Swedish Scientist, Van Der Vaal.

4. Thalaathalam: Layers of Plates, from metal/metal alloys, formed at different temperature ranges.

5. Ma(h)kithalam: The stratum formed with Ma(h)ki – Graphite, which can withstand temperatures at 3,000 and above (as per Present Scientific information), compounded with Kalnaar-Abestos. This stratum is so hard that it can hold Plates upon itself. Asbestos is a thermal insulator, insulating from the super heated metals contained under this stratum, forming itself as the shell.

6. Irasa thalam Irasam-Concentrate. Super heated metals, unable to melt or expand, because of the shell formation of Ma(h)kithalam and compressed within, leading to great pressure. Several metals form this stratum, partially expanded and molten, in the grooves formed by uneven thickness of Mahithalam..

The molten ones flows like serpentine rivers, with branches, also as rivers, and small branches, termed as their "babies". These are termed, Irasathala Aravukal.(Aravukal - serpents).

These are seismic lines, as it is called today. In Vall(h)uvam, that whenever these tried to play with their babies, Nila Athirvu - earthquakes occur, meaning that, when slight alignments happened because of high pressure due to high temperature, earthquakes occured.. There are eight 'Aravu's' mentioned to be existing. Two of them, known are detailed below. (Routes and places furnished refers to what is known to us today to facilitate understanding.

(1) Vaasuki: Almost in line with Visuvathanam (Equator), encircling the earth, and is also very powerful. It is south of the Date-line marked by Mayans, and starting from here, extended to Kaandava vanam (in the middle of Bay of Bengal – submerged about 5,100 years ago), passed through its branched out islands (Andaman, Indonesia, Philippines, Central Pacific islands, Central American countries, and ends at the staring point.

(2) Karakoram: commences from the eastern side of the Date Line, passes through Atlantic, with a rever-like branch towards north, linking several islands (Bermuda), and the main one (Karakoram) passing through Salt sea (Mediterranean), mountain/hills north of Salathi Kadal, i.e., Black Sea and Caspian sea, which were once a single sea before the Deluge, that rocked the world, about 5,100 years ago), passed through the passage between Imaya kootam (Himalayas, as is known today), through Ila velhi, i.e., northern China Gobi desert, and Mongolian territories, and after entering the Eastern Perunkadal (Pacific) turned Northeast- ward (though Japan), and ended in North East point of the Panipparai land (Alaska).

[Note: Four natural serpentine formations are mentioned, viz., 1) Whirlwind and tornadoes, 2) whirlpools in rivers, 3)

Lava flowing through in Vithalam, and 4) Serpentine seismic lines in Irasa thalam]..

7) Paathaalam: Paatha-Deeply embedded, which cannot be redeemed; Thalam-Stratum. This forms the core of the Earth. This consists of

various metals/non metals, and as they are super heated, and cannot expand or melt, they remain under great Pressure. Whatever that could expand and partially melted, has formed the Irasa Thalam, which surrounds it.

Details of Planets, yielded by the Sun, which are under its control, are as below.

1) **Sani – Saturn**: San- Subservient (to the Sun)+ E-Iyam – function; The Planet exists in tne last Range of the Axial Control of Sun and circumambulates the Sun). The Sanskrit word "Sanaischaram" referring to this planet, interpreted as 'the one that moves slowly'. This nomenclature is only a variant of Thamizh term, but the interpretation is a misnomer).
Proper Sanskrit Term - **"Gayathri"**.

Based on Vall(h)uvam:

Distance from Sun – 905.3 Million Miles. (1445.8 million K.Ms.)
Age – 1885 Crore Years -18.85 billion years.
Time taken to circumambulate the Sun – 30 years (10,800 days).

Present Scientific Data:
Distance from Sun – 886.5 Million miles.
Time taken to circumambulate Sun – 10,752.22 days.(29 years, 9 months, and 3.22 days)
Temperature – (-) 180 degrees Celsious.
Moons (Satellite Planets) – 10.

- - - - - -

2. **Viyaazhan** – **Jupitor**: The name implies that all the activities have ceased, because of the three basic ingredients for organic activities, viz., Appu-Hydrogen, Asu-Oxygen and Kari-carbon were all compounded with metals and non metals and lying as dusts, and also that its core had cooled down such that no activity can be revived in it.

Sanskrit Term: "**Ushnik**", that is. the thermal activities had ceased.

Vall(h)uvam:

Age of the Planet from the date of its formation in the Sun. -- 7,560 Million years. (756 Crore Years).

Distance from Sun – 479 Million miles (966.4 million K.Ms).

Time taken for circumambulating the Sun: 12 yrs, and 4 days..:(4320 days).

Present Scientific Data:

Distance from Sun – 486 Million Miles.

Time taken tocircumambulatng the Sun -4332.59 days (12 yrs and 16.59 dys)

Temperature – (-) 123 degrees Celcius.

Moons – 16.

- - - - - -

3) Chevvai – Mars:

Erintha sambal nirainthu Uyirthal Atra Puvi – The surface is filled with Burnt ashes, and subsequent non existence of Life system.

Life system developed through evolution, ended, as the shell surrounding the Core of this planet cracked, metals in captivated in the Core, burst out with great force, resulting in absorbing the Carbon, Nitrogen, Hydrogen and

Oxygen, forming oxides, hydrates, etc., resulting in annihilation of life system. The Term, "Chevvai" is based on the above theory.

Sanskrit Term: **Bruhathi.**

Vall(h)uvam: Age up to date – 930 Million years.

Distance from Sun: - 120 Million Miles. (192 Million KMs.)

Time taken for circumambulation of Sun: 679 days (1 Year, 10 Months and 19 days).

Present Scientific Data:

Distance from Sun – 145 Million Miles.

Time taken to circumambulate the Sun: -686.98 days.

1 year, 10 months and 26 days)

No of Moons – 2.

- - - - - -

4) **Puvi, Pookol(h)am and also Pankthi.** – Earth and also Globe):

Various details regarding the Earth have already been furnished. While The Sun is denoted as (G)nyaayiru, as his performance is agreeable to all the planets, Life system on the Earth is performing, in line with Sun, and as such called (G)nyaalam.

Some more particulars regarding the Earth.

Vall(h)uvam

Age of he Earth – 842.4 Million Years.

Distance from Sun: at Kataka Iraasi Varai(Line 0f Cancer) -95.6 Million Miles.

At Makara Iraasi Varai (Line of Capricorn – 92.6 MillionMiles.

Time taken to circumambulating the Sun – Days- 365; Orais-6 and Vinaatis -59, and Naatis -4, i.e., 365 days, 6 hours 23 minues and 40 seconds.

Present ScientificData:

Distace from Sun – 92.9 million Miles. Time teken for Circumambulaion – 365.26 days.

Temperature -22 degrees Celsius.

Moon – 1.

- - - - - -

5) **Nilaa - Moon:** Nila – Steady, i.e., without rotation. Also termed upakolh, as it circumambulates the Earth on its Anuvattom as its satellite, being induced by the Earth's Axial Control..

It is also referred to by several other names, viz., Thinkal, Udupan (travels around earth, without any activity on its own), Anu Udupan (travels under the prime control of Earth), The word "Pirai" means aperture, aperture of moon as seen from Earth as waxing and vaning moon.

It travels at a very great Velocity, viz., slightly above 63,000 KMs an hour Because of this, it gains para magnetic field around its atmosphere, enabling it to obtain its own Gravitational force, and linking with Earth's Gravitational force.

Vall(h)uvam:-

Age of Nilaa is the same as the Earth.

Diatance from earth – As its 'Anuvattom trajectory varies in four paths, it comes closer to earth during some period, at 200,000 Kms., but generally it is 300,00 Kms..

Time taken to circumambulate the Earth – 353/354 days. It is standardised to some extent, once in every 80 years.

No. of months for 80 Years, as per Samvacchara year of earth is 960, whereas, for Anuvacchara year calculations relating to moon is 1,000 months, thereby there is additional 40 months.

For Samvacchara calculation, taking into account one additional day for every four years, and with reference to Moon (Anuvaccharam), increases by 12 to 15 days. As stars are stable because of the distance from Earth, the time and positions of the Moon are calculated with reference to the stars and the place/position on Earth.

- - - - - -

6) **Vellhi – Venus**:-

Similar to Moon of the earth, this planet also was formed at the outer periphery of the core of the Sun, and is circumam- bulating on its own Trajectory, as a moon to the Sun. It rises in horizon in the early morning and reflects Sun's light over the earth. The Thamizh nomenclature itself that it lightens (twilight) the earth.

Vall(h)uvam:
Age of the Planet – 517.6 million years.
Distance from Sun – 69 million miles (112 million Kms.)
Time taken to circumambulate the Sun – 228 days.(7 months and 18 days).

Present Scientific Data: Distance fom Sun – 67 million miles.
Time taken for circumambulating the Sun: -224.7 days.
Temperature – 480 degrees Celsius.

- - - - - -

7) **Puthan – Mercury**:

Thamizh Name means, the newly formed one.

Just like Vellhi (Venus) this planet was also formed at outer periphery of the Sun's core. And circumambulates the Sun, just as its Moon.

Vall(h)uvam:

Age of the Planet – 325 million Years.

Distance from the Sun – 46 million miles. (705 Kms).

Circumambulating time – 89 days.

Present Scientific Data:

Disance from Sun – 35 million miles.

Circumambulating time -87.9 days.

Temperature – 520degrees Celsius.

Its Trajectory: (Vall(h)uvam): While the Earth's trajectory is elongated from Makara Iraasi (Line of Capricorn), towards Kataka Iraasi (Line of Cancer), that of Puthan (mercury) is varied by 90 degrees. (With reference to the Earth, it is elongated from Me(y)ta Iraasi to Thulaa Iraasi). Therefore, the distance from Sun has to be assessed in two different positions).

[Note: Followers of Religious scriptures, while performing obeisance three times, at sunrise, midday, and sunset, sit and mention the names of those spread as 7 configurations, viz.,

(i)   mention the name of seven Rishis, touching the head:
      Athri, Bhrugu, Kuthsa, Vasishta, Gouthama, Kaashyapa and Angirasa,

(ii) seven planets, touching the nose; - Gayathri (Sani – Saturn), Ushnik (Viyazhan-Jupitor), Bhruhathi(Chevvai-Mars), Pankthi (same as

Thamizh name, referring to Puvi-Earth), Anushtup(Phonetic variant of Thamizh name –Anu Udupan, i.e., Nila – Moon), Thrushtup (Velli-Venus), and, Jagathi (Puthan- Mercury).

(iii) Touching the Naval point, Agni, Vaayu, Arka, Vakeesa, Varuna, Indra Viswa. Deva devathaas.

Let us take up the Group (ii). (1) Gayathri- Sani: Though the Sanskrit name of Saturn is 'Gayathri', while in Astrology, they refer this planet with Thamizh name, Sani. According to them Gayathri is a Goddess, i.e., manifesting, Parvathi Lakshmi and Saraswathi, and as such worshipable, and as for Sani (Saturn), while the Sun has given birth to Yama as the eldest, a holy one, who is the Ruler of Dharma (Code of life), and Kaalam(time), he has given birth to himself -Sani- the younger, as lame. Because of this, he is inimical towards the God, Sun, and, therefore he is evil. In Sanskrit Astrology, they use only the Tamil nomenclature.

2) Though Viyazhan – Jupitor is referred to as Ushnik they have coined out a new name, "Guru", i.e., Guru of Indhra Deva.

3) Chevvai – Mars is denoted as Bhruhathi in Sanskrit, which refers to Bhruhaspati, Guru of Indhra Deva, they refer to it as "Angaarakan", i.e., Burnt ash, the present status. While the original name implies it as a respectable and holy one, by the astrological name, they find it unholy.

4) As for the seventh planet-Mercury, the Sanskrit nomenclature-Jagathi-itself implies, "Just born and is in process of life", They use the phonetic variant of Thamizh word-Puthan', viz., Bhudha.

The nomenclatures of two celestial events, viz., Ira(h)ku(Solar eclipse) and Kethu(Lunar eclipse), are also added as Planets, and declared Nava Grahas (Nine Planets).

The above are only a few to show that Astrology is at variance with Astronomy, even though it is claimed that it is also a 'science'.

Solar system. Beyond six Planets under the orbital control of the Sun, three other Planets, viz., Neptune, Pluto and Uranus, are out of orbital of Sun. There are very many such planets discovered by Astro Scientists. Such planets without orbital controls are termed "widowed Planets"

CHAPTER 9

Stars –Stellar Galaxy

The nomenclature for Star in Thamizh is,'Natchathram. This word is defined as below: Nal(h) –Fulcrum; Chathiram-unvarying capability. Thus it is the fulcrum of the planets yielded by it, and is capable of controlling them. Several of the stars form a complex, termed as Natchathira Mandalam; these Mandalams form Natchathira Kootam, i.e., 'Galaxy. (In Sanskrit Star is called, "Thara". And Galaxy is termed 'Samsthanam').

When looked above the head from North Pole, the Kootam – Galaxy- is in the shape of a fish rising above into the sky, with Thiruva Natchathiram as the base and Thiruvonam (Thiru+Onam) at the top of its nose. As such the Kootam – Galaxy was termed a "Vinnh Meen", i.e., "the Stellar Fish."

[Note: The Pandiya King Malayavan, who ruled from Mathurai about 12,500 years ago, decorated this Stellar Fish as his Insignia on his flag. This Mathurai city was submerged into sea during the Deluge/Catastrophe that rocked the World about 5,100 years go. The plateau of this City, remains as 'Mathura island, northeast of Jawa and northwest of Bali island of Indonesia as a historical monument.]

The whole Galaxy looks stable because of the distance. But they are whirling round, slowly drifting towards the edge of the Universe, surrounded by the Cosmic Waves. This Natural process is termed as "karoodam"; Ka-kadathal – passing away, roodam-rotation. (When mentioned as a Term,

Urudam -rolling and Urulai is the material that rolls – Roller) the Sanskrit word, 'Garuda' is a Phonetic variant of the Thamizh word.

[Note: The name of the ancient land, now called 'Egypt', was "Salmali". It is an indicative Thamizh word, since it implies that 'Sal' trees were abundant (malindu-abundantly). It was also mentioned that Salmaliers, the people of that landscape, worshipped Garuda. Even today there are ancient temples, dating back to about 7,000 years, protected as Monuments. These are Tourist attractions, and the people of that Country announce that their ancestors the worshiped the God as "O Goruda", phonetic variant of "Om Garuda".

Salmaliers were ethnically a separate entity, different from Yavana (Italy, Greece, Portugal, France Ireland and western part of Turkey), Gandharva (northern Europe), Yootha(Jews) of Western part of middle East, Arabians, Barbarians (migrants in Libya and Algeria – Originally termed 'Barbars' originated from the landscape East/south east of "Pamirs"; They were Mongols, i.e., yellow skinned people. (Mongol is a phonetic variant of Thamizh word-Manjal, i.e., Yellow), Kimpurusha –Gypsy. It may be noted that the names, 'Solomon, salomy, Salmon, etc., are all from the word "salmaliers].

(Galaxy – contd.)

One portion of the stellar constellations are visible at night when Iravi (Sunlight) traverses from Makara Iraasi towards northern hemisphere, while the other portion can be seen at night, when Iravi traverses from Kataka Iraasi towards southern Hemisphere. The stellar constellations are named by their appearances. They are noted as 27 constellations, on the 12 Iraasi kattoms (blocks), during each of which they are predominant. As the Star Thiruva with the stars, Apichith and Arunthathi, can be seen on all nights (Thiruva as the Pole Star to locate the northern direction), they are not marked in Iraasi Kattoms.

```
        [--(1)*_____
   [ 12]   1 ]   2 ]   3  ]
   [   ]     ]     ]      ]____(2)*
   [ 11]   Iraasi   [   4  ]
   [   ]   kattam  [      ]
   [ 10 ]          [   5  ]
(4)*-[   ]          [      ]
   [ 9 ]   8 ]   7 ]   6 ]
   [   ]     ]     ]      ]
                  ]—(3)*
```

*Four Sankaramanams (Equinoxes).(1)-Metam-eqinox at Equator –first day of New Year. (2) Katakam-Equinox at Line of Cancer–commencement of 4th month. (3) Thula- 2nd equinox at equator –commencement of 7th month. (4) Makaram-Equinox at Line of Capricorn commencement of 10th month

Each Iraasi kattam denotes a month, and mark of Iravi in the Kattam denotes the respective month. (Iravi –Sunrise and its light starts pervading over the Earth). Each Constellation is divided into 4 paadas (Paadam – is foot, i.e., walk or passage. Here it is interpreted as four divisions. Each month is of 30 degrees,

Iravi, covers this angular positions denoting the day of the month in which it is marked. Nine divisions of the constellations are marked in each Kattam, related to Iravi (here, the date) denotes the time.

It is generally known, while time is assessed with reference to the Sun's position, at night the time is assessed by the positions of the division of Constellation. in respect of the month and date. It is mentioned that 'persons travelled/went to any place, were guided by the Stars during night, to know the time and directions.. Even today there are people, mostly tribal people, follow this practice. Ships were guided at night by Pole star for navigation.

The twelve Iraasi kattams denote 12 months beginning with first month, Chithirai. In these 9 padams i.e., divisions [at 4 divisions for each constellation] of the stellar constellations are marked as below:

1st month –Chithirai; Asuvathi(4), Apparani(4), Kaarthikai-1st paadam. (April 14-May 14).

2nd –Vaikaasi –Kaarthikai-2, 3, & 4 paadams, Urokini, Maarkaseram-1,2 paadams. (May 15 - June 15).

3rd –Aani: Maarkaseeram- 3,4 paadams. Thiru Athirai, Punarpoosam- 1, 2, 3 Paadams.(June 16-July 16).

4th –Aati: Punarpoosam-1st paadam, Poosam, Aayilium. (July17 – August 15).

5th – Aavani: Makam, pooram, Uthiram -1st Paadam (August 16 - September 16).

6th- Purattasi: Uthiram -2,3,4 paadams, Attham, Chithirai-1,2 Paadams. (September 17-October 16)

7th – Ayipasi: Chithirai-3,4, Suvaathi. Visakam-1,2,3 Paadams (October 17th-November 15th).

8th- Kaarthikai: Visakam—4th, Anusam, Kettai.(November 16th –December 14th).

9th Maarkazhi: Moolam, pooraadam, Uthiraadam-1st Paadam. (December 15th January 13th).

10th Thai: Uthiraadam- 2,3,4 Paadams, Thiru Onam, Avittam-1,2paadams.(January 14th-February 12th)

11th Maasi: Avittam -3,4 paadams Sathayam, Poorattathi -1,2,3 Paadams (February 13th -March 13th)

12th Panguni: Poorattathi -4th Paadams, Utirattathi. Revathi. (March 14th –April 13th).

Saayanam: This is dependent on Idavaccharam (rotation of Earth on its own Axis), to calculate the variations of Naazhikai 24 minute – unit time), Details from Chithirai are furnished below:

1st: 4-1/4, 2nd:4-1/4, 3rd: 5-1/4. 4th: 5-1/2, 5th: 5-1/4, 6th:5, 7th: 5, 8th: 5-1/4, 9th: 5-1/2, 10th: 5-1/4, 11th: 4-1/4, an 12th: 4-1/4.

These figures are to calculate the beginning of each month with reference to Iravi (Sunrise) at Naazhikai Vattil (Circular Time Chamber at Kaandava Vanam Island), and the Date Line (at Mexico). These calculations are can be analysed as follows:

Kaala Thiruk Kanitham (Almanac) for every year is computed by several Vithakars (specialists) at least a year or two before, compared/verified among themselves and finalised. The following details regarding Solar/Lunar Eclipses for 2012 -2013 AD., as per Kala Thiruk kanitham, are furnished below:

During this year, two Iraahku kaalams (Solar Eclipses), and two Kethu Kaalams (Lunar Eclipses) will occur

Ira(h)ku Kaalam (Solar Eclipse):

1) 20-5-2012 (Sunday). The timing and altitudinal/ Latitudinal positions are such that this cannot be seen in India.
2) 13-11-2012 (Tuesday); 28th Ayipasi – Suvathi Star; This does no appear in India.

Kethu Kaalam (LunarEclpse)

1) 4-6-2012 Monday); Will not appear in India.
2) 28-12-2012 (Wednesday): 13th, Kaarthikai
   Month-Will not appear in India.

CHAPTER 10

Other systems of Date-Year calculations followed in The World.

Solar Calendar followed by theWestern World:

Pope Gregory Paul-I, adopted the Calendar, of the Jews for Christian Laity to follow. He set 1st January as the year beginning. This is normally known as Anglo year in India. Hereafter we shall refer to this as Western Calendar.

[Note: The two juxtaposed Triangles is the national Insignia of the Jews, is the same one the Mayans denoted as the commencement of Time – Parama An(h)ukaalam.]

According to this Calendar, the date on which the Beam of Sunlight is exactly on Equator on March 21. When the Sunlight is on the South of Equator, the light falls on Earth leniently. Refraction takes place, when it enters Ozone layer, again when it enters Ionosphere, and, finally when it enters the atmosphere, the third refraction takes place. Thereby, it looks as though the Sunlight falls straight above Equator. It was assessed by Mayans, that these refractions cover 6 Iraasi varai's (Latitude). As 4 days for a Iraasi, it works out to 24 days. Therefore, they fixed April 14, as the beginning of new year.]

Palestine was mentioned in Srimadh Bhagavatham (compiled before about 5,100 Years) as "Palasa Dweepam', where Yoothas lived. Yoothas mean Tribes, and it refers to Jews, as they are known today.

Palestine and the Western countries, are situated above 25 Iraasi varai (Latitude), and, therefore, daytime is not uniform throughout the year. But, they can see the Sun straight at mid-day. Based on this, they have taken mid night as Day-break, and accordingly, their calendar was also computed. Western Countries including the Gregorian calendar follow this. Moreover, Greenwich (U.K.) is marked as "Zero degree" Latitude, and time calculations follow this. For them, Date-line is at far Pacific.

Earlier, they took 365 days for a Year. Later, only in 1200 A.D., they found out that there is a lag of 6 hours a year, and added one day to the month of February, and called it Leap Year. Thereafter, Leap Year came into force. This was in vogue in Samvacchara calendar from ancient times.

In Samvacchara Year, the year of the Earth increases at one Naati (Second) for every 20 years. As such, as time passed, it accumulated to 23 minutes, 40 seconds as on date, which is rounded off as one Naazhikai (24 minutes) for every year This additional Time Lag is accounted every year, and one day is added to the year after every 60 years. This was accepted by the Western scientists recently. But, in 2010/2011, when one day was added in Samvacchara calendar, this was not added in Gregorian calendar, as it was felt that it would entail various complications in accounting, etc...

Chapter 11

Lunar Calendar (Chandramana Yugathi), followed by Soma sect:

Northern part of China is Gobi Desert. This and nearby areas, referred to as Eelaaveli (Eelaavrutham in Sanskrit) is the abode of Mongols, the yellow coloured people. Mongol is the phonetic variant of Tamizh word, 'Manchal', meaning Yellow.

They worship, Sankaran, inThamizh, i.e. Sankarshanah in Sanskrit, which is personified as many headed Cobra (Adi Sesha) on which Lord Vishnu is reclining. This one is taken as "The Dragon" in cultural processions by Chinese.

This area is situated above Iraasi Varai (Latitude)40-45 degrees, Sun could be viewed from South East to South West only throughout the year. During Northern Trajectory of Iravi (Sunlight), Day time increased gradually, and, when the Beam of Sunlight fell on Line of Cancer directly, practically it would be day- time for the major portion of the day and night time would be minimal. Similarly, when the Sunlight traverses towards the Line of Capricorn, there would be only twilight for few days before, and on the day the Sunlight fell on that Line. There would be no Daytime and only twilight would be spread in these areas.

On January 14th, when Sunlight commences Journey on Northern Trajectory, there would be the display of **Aura,** i.e., it would be Crimson red and orange light on the Southern Horizon, for a few seconds, during the middle of the Day. The Mongols celebrated this Celestial display. Subsequent to this, on the next 3rd Day of the waxing moon their Lunar New year began.

[Note: The Mongols, who have migrated and settled in the western part of South India (Now called Kerala), declared a hill on the Western Ghats as Sabarimla, has given religious colour, and display this Aura event with a torch behind a hill in the evening, after Sun-set, as "Makara Jothi". Since there would be bright Sunlight during mid-day, they changed the event to evening to suit their religious fervor. That day is the harvest festival in the South, and, for that matter, the day is celebrated as Makara Sankaranthi throughout the country. Lot of people, even educated, have left off their customary harvest festival and flock here to watch the pseudo event.]

Aura observed at Northern China/Mongolia on January 14ᵗʰ for a few seconds in Southern Horizon, when the Beam of Sunlight commences its traverse towards North.

Lunar Year (Sanskrit: Chandramaana Ugadi):

As the Sun woul not be visible throughout the year, as explained in the earlier paragraphs, and, as they could view the Moon on all days of the year they followed the Moon's trajectory- Anu vattom, for the Year calculations.

Moon would be visible only from the third Waxing Moon, they took that day as the first day of every Month.

(According to a section of them, who called the present Pamir knot (Tajikistan) as "Sumeru", the tuft of Lord Shiva. As they watched the third Waxing Moon on this knot, and as such, they declared that the aperture (Pirai in Thamizh and Mouli in Sanskrit) decorates His tuft of hair.).

Though the Moon is directly related the Axial contol of the Earth, its trajectory is influenced by the Sun's Gravity also. Therefore, its trajectory is not set to a methodical path with reference to the Earth's Equator, and is varying, covering both Northern and Southern Hemispheres of the Earth. Due to this it takes 24 hrs and 51 minutes to circumambulate the Earth once a day.

(This is approximate and varies depending on its trajectory). Thus it takes 51 minutes more than the day of the Earth, i.e., 24 hours. On New Moon's Day, the Moon arises along with Sun and sets at 6-25 PM. Hence, it cannot be viewed in Sunlight on that day. The third waxing Moon alone can be sighted over the hills (Sumeru) at 8-12 PM.(approximate), and, therefore, the Chinese took 3rd Waxing Moon as the beginning of each Month.

[Note: Lunar calendar is followed as Hijiri by Muslims and also by Somavamsa people, who have migrated from China and the Middle East, including Afganisthan.

Chinese. observed their New Year from the Third Waxing Moon, which falls after the day on which the Sun-light commences its traverse from the Line of Capricorn towards North, mostly falling in January itself.

Muslims followed the 3rd Waxing Moon as the beginning of each Month. Their Hijiri Year commences from the 3rd Waxing Moon in the month of November.

Soma Vamsha People, who have migrated to India, took the New Moon Day as the beginning of each month and their Year commences from the New Moon Day, which falls in March/April. Though they have changed the month-beginning to New Moon Day (Sanskrit-Amavasya), they still consider sighting the 3rd waxing Moon as auspicious.]

Some of the examples regarding the variations of Lunar Trajectory are furnished below:

1) 2010-2011: Lunar Year- 355 days, 23 hours, 41 minutes – 356 days approximately. This is lesser by 9 days to the Standard Earth's Year (Solar year) 0f 365 days.

2) 2011-2012: Lunar Year – 353 days, 19 hours, 4 minutes, Further, addition of one day in 2012, being a Leap year, is not accounted. Thus, there is the difference, lesser, by 11 days.

3) 2012-2013: 387 days. This was arrived at, by totalling the differences in the previous two years, i.e., 20 days, and also the number of days that would accrue during this year. They skipped the New Moon that would fall by February end, and took the next one that fell in April of that year.

The New Year day is called Ugadi by the SomaVamsha people in India.

(Many of those, settled in Tamil Nadu and Kerala States, have taken to Samvacchara calendar, to go in line with the local people.).

The above figures are furnished only to understand the Lunar year calculations.

According to this System, 1,000 Months will be completed in 80 years, thereby, 40 months, i.e., 3 years and 4 months more than 960 months of Samvacchara as well as Solar systems. This amounts to 12-1/2 months of Lunar calendar to 12 months of standard. Year, i.e. 14-1/2 days of days more every year, i.e., 365-14-1/2=350-1/2 days. Since a day is added every leap year, amounting to 20 days, it adds up to 2-1/2 days a year. Adding this to 350-1/2 days, it amounts to 353 days a Year.

Moreover, in Lunar calendar, the Year cycle is 80 years, and, therefore, every year is denoted as incomplete year for 79 years and in the 80th year the cycle is complete. By this account, they have named each incomplete year and have also predicted, based on these names. This year, relating to 2013, is denoted as serpent's year.

(SomaVamshis in India too, by Celebrationg 'Sathabhishekam' when one completes 80 years age.)

CHAPTER 12

Creation from the Core of Nature.

Let us take up Creation of Mass from the Core of Nature.

This is dealt with in Aaya Kalai Mupperunmai (Treatise on Tri-Ordeal Theory) in Thamizh language, and later translated to Sanskrit and termed, Thathva Thrayam. The period, during which these Great truths were rendered, is not known but was only referred to Kaasyapa's Madapusi Ashramam. Reference was made to Chitthar Kaasyapar in the earlier Chapter dealing with Creation and Evolution of Earth under "Manvanthira Kaalam".

In the first Psalm of "Pallandu", Vishnu Chitthan Kone, popularly known as "Periaalwar", King of Seervilliputhur (4-3rd Centuryv B.C.), has referred to the Core of Nature as "Mal-Aanda Thinh Tholh Manivnnaa",

'Mal' has dual interpretation: 1) m+al. m-mass/matter, and al-Allaatha-Devoid, The one devoid of mass for itself; 2) mal-Strength (of Wrestler-Mallan). As both are apt, mal-Aaanda –Controls/Rules. Thus the phrase, 'Mal-Aanda Thinh' implies: The Thinh, devoid of mass and Rules over the strength (of Wrestler), refers to Potential Energy (Omni Potent).

Tholh – Shoulder - the one that shoulders all that created. It Carries another interpretation: Thaa (n)+ulh; thaan –The all pervading one, on its own, ulh- within. Thus, The all pervading one that involves on its own (Omniscient and Omnipotent).

Man(h)ivann(h)a: Man(h)i –Pure Diamond, which is not visible, such that even light cannot be reflected, and passes through without any obstruction;

Vann(h)a –Concerning mass, it is vann(h)am - form/shape.. As it has no mass it is not confined to dimension/shape, i.e., colourless.

Thus the core of Nature, is depicted as the one Omnipotent, that rules (Controls) over the strength, involve on is own as Omniscient and Omnipresent, is not bound by any dimensional characters, as All Pervading, which cannot be noticed, felt nor hold.

The Core is mentioned by different names, each one a definition in itself. Some of them are,

Karu (Core)- In mass it is Karumai, i.e., Black and also as a "Hole", as it cannot be revealed by light.. Hence, It is defined as, the one that is Hallow like Black. The present definition as "Black Hole" is synonymous.

Thiru – As a mass it means thirutham, i.e., Blemishless, but referring to the Karu it means "Absolute".

Azh – In mass it is termed Alh, i.e. basis of limitations. But the word Azh is the one not bound by limitations, and all-pervading.

Akaran – "Prime one" as the first alphabet – A to any language (A pronounced as in 'at').

Thuzhai – Search. In this context - "the one that cannot be felt or seen".

Karu (Core) is "individual self" without anything else in company, and, as such, it is defined as 'Than' (Pronounced just as That), meaning, 'On its own'. It being the prime base for all creations is also denoted as 'Ath'.

As 'Ath', it enables the prime stage of creation and takes the first and primary position, viz., Athi (Ath –Prime self+ I - Iyal, i.e., Enablement).

Ath –initiates as the Prime one, and this stage is mentioned as Aathi (A+Athi).

1) Initiation: There are three words defining action, viz., 'Utthu' -self priming, 'Unthu' –Induce, and, 'Thoondu'- instigate.

As there is no mass, Ath takes to self priming and as Aathi, primes within itself and transforms as 'Azhuthu'.

This action in mass is denoted as Azhutham, meaning Pressure, specifically, 'Vacuum Pressure'.

In the present context, as the Karu is Absolute, the term, Azhuthu can be defined as "Absolute Vacuum Pressure".

Just as the water, when heated, vapour rises initially little by little, because of Azuthu minute Blue-black Waves evolve, rises above, and, beyond a position, encircle and vivisect a portion of Karu in a spherical form. (Encirclement –Chuzhal in Thamizh)

At the inner level, close to the pressure point, the waves are of microscopic frequency, beyond the level of our imagination. As the distance grow at the outer periphery, the frequencies reduces, thereby form a Range of these Blue-black Waves. As they are hair-like, each one independent of the other, they are termed, Kesava alaikal (alaikal-waves. Kesam – Hair on head).

As these are evolved from Aathi stage of Karu, Karu is depicted as "Aathi Kesava", and also Kaari, meaning the one that caused this Initiation.

2) Second stage of initiation: Once the Blue-Black waves are evolved and set itself into action by self priming, Karu, i.e., Thinh, being potential Energy, transforms into "Thiran", i.e., Kinetic Energy.

As Thinh is the Prime Place, in which Blue-black Waves vivisected the Sphere, it is termed **"An(h)tam".** (Itam – Place)

AN(H)AVAM: To process activities further, Thin(h) takes Prime position – An(h); and takes prime responsibity on its own – Av, and also being the Prime factor for creation of mass –Am. All the above three factors are combined and termed "An(h)avam". Anavam (an(h)avam) is the Vithi –Formula. As the initiation of Thiran-Kinetic Energy is of the Wave form, the formula, An(h)avam can be explained with the present Scientific term, Harmonics. To understand this, it is elaborated by the Sound, "OOH(M)", where, 'M' is the nasal depiction. "Conch" is the personification to establish this Theory of Harmonics. When the conch is blown, the sound emanates from it is not dampened, and as it is continuous, the frequency of the sound is doubled, which is doubled again and so on in Geometric progression.

As the distance grow at the outer periphery, the frequencies reduces, thereby form a Range of these Blue-black Waves. As they are hair-like, each one independent of the other, they are termed, Kesava alaikal (alaikal-waves. Kesam – Hair on head).

As these are evolved from Aathi stage of Karu, Karu is depicted as "Aathi Kesava", and also Kaari, meaning the one that caused this Initiation.

2) Second stage of initiation: Once the Blue-Black waves are evolved and set itself into action by self priming, Karu, i.e., Thinh, being potential Energy, transforms into "Thiran", i.e., Kinetic Energy.

CHAPTER 13

An(h)tam and An(h)avam

As Thinh is the Prime Place, within which, Blue-black Waves encircled within the Core and vivisected a Spherical portion, which is termed **"An(h) tam".**(Itam – Place)

AN(H)AVAM: To process activities further, Thin(h) takes Prime position – An(h); and takes prime responsibity on its own – Av, and also being the Prime factor for creation of mass –Am. All the above three factors are combined and termed "An(h)avam". Anavam (an(h)avam) is the Vithi –Formula. As the initiation of Thiran-Kinetic Energy is of the Wave form, the formula, An(h)avam can be explained with the present Scientific term, **Harmonics.** To understand this, it is elaborated by the Sound, "OOH(M)", where, 'M' is the nasal depiction. "Conch" is the personification to establish this Theory of Harmonics. When the conch is blown, the sound emanates from it is not dampened, and as it is continuous, the frequency of the sound is doubled, which is doubled again and so on in Geometric progression.

Same way the sound reduces itself into half, which is again halved, in the Geometric Regression.

Note: The An(h)ava Vithi is observed as a Ritual in The Narayur Nambi Temple at Nacchiyar Koil Town (Original name-Thiru Narayiur), few Kilometers west of Kumbakonam (original name –Kudanthai) in Tamil Nadu). The ritual is as follows:

When the Deity is taken in a procession, the palanquin is carried by 4 persons up to the Main Entrance Kopuram (Temple Tower). When the procession turns to North from the Tower, 4x2 - 8 persons carry it. When it turns and passes through North street, it is carried by 8x2 - 16 persons. When the procession turns to south and proceed through East Street, 16x2 - 32 persons carry it. After turning to South and passes through South Street, it is carried by 32x2 - 64 persons, Finally when procession turns from South street towards the Temple, it is carried by 64x2 – 128 persons. Though the procession is awe inspiring with devotion, the message is wonderful, when the purport of the depiction is understood.

[Soma Vamshis prefixed 'pr' and pronounce it as Pranavam in Sanskrit Their explanation to this is that the first alphabets of three Vedas, viz., A+u+m forms Om, (Aum-linked to groaning during sexual act) and it was imparted to Purooravasu at the beginning of Thretha Yuga, when he was wandering in Agnisthala, i.e., Arabian Desert, when his mind was engrossed in the thought of Urvasi, a Court Dancer in Indra Loka.. Their depiction narrated in 8th Canto of Srimad Bhagavatam (Soma Vamsha) is atrocious, and devoid of any reasoning, and, therefore, irrelevant. Moreover, "pr" is the base for Prasavam –Birth, which is also irrelevant].

CHAPTER 14

Universe and evolution thereon.

This Universe is also one such Antam. It is termed Vikuntam, i.e., vi-vithikappatta, i.e., established, as kuntam - sphere.

Azh took upon itself as a Shell under the Blue-Black Waves, such that these Waves could not enter in and pervade.

Azh then took up the responsibility as "Azhi" to enable creation and evolution within the Kuntam. (Azh +e –Enable). This nomenclature also means, 'fence'. to the Kuntam, within.

As the Blue-Black waves were initiated as kinetic Energy, they induced the evolution of Waves within Azhi. These waves were of various ranges, and independent of each other, just as hair. These waves are termed "Visuva Thevam". Visu –oscillation; va - vaham – taking upon itself, i.e., as waves. These are, what is today referred to as "Cosmic Waves".

Highest range of these waves starts encircling next to Azhi within the Kuntam. Lower range of Visuva Thevam encircled below the highest ones.

The first one is termed as 'Chayan' (Cha –righteous, and Ya –function), i.e., the one that functions righteously without deviation.

The second one is termed, 'Vichayan', i.e., vi- virivu i.e.,

Expansive (fanning out) +chayan, i.e., these waves were far away from Azhi and also lesser in the wave range, turned and entered the Space within the Kuntam.

These two together are called, Guardians of the Entrance, such that no mass nor Waves could enter Azhi.

The space in which these waves are evolved is referred to as

'Thapa Ulakam'. Tha- of own self; pa –hold Ula- Ulavu –roam; ka- pass through its destined activity.

The Space within it is referred to as Aazhi. (Aa is pronounced as in 'auction'), the space within which greater activities, other than traverse, commence. Azhi established Anhavam (Harmonics) as the formula, and, thereupon Azhi, the Shell was termed "Vaikuntam" (Vithi- establishment of the formula; vihitham – various forms and divisions +kuntam, i.e., The one that caused the establishment of An(h)avam for creation of various forms and divisions.

By An(h)ava vithi (harmonics) Waves of lesser frequencies evolved from the Chaya and Vichaya Thevams (Cosmic Waves), mainly, Olhi alaikal (Light waves) (Alaikal- plural of Alai-Waves), and these waves were passing throughout the Aazhi(Space) as Rays. As there was no mass initially, the light waves could not manifest on their own. Therefore, eventhough there was light throughout, Aazhi was not revealed and was contained within itself. This stage of Aazhi was denoted as "Chudar Aazhi". (Chudar- the light which is contained within self).

To sum up, Azh, as Akaran (Self Priming), caused the initiation of 'Thiran' (Kinetic Energy), in the form of Blue- Black Waves, and further, caused vivisection of self, when these waves encircled, resulting in formation of An(h) tam, i.e., the placement of Anh (Potenial energy).

Azh then took upon self as Azhi, (the shell), fence, within An(h)tam. Azhi, then, induced the formation of Visuva Thevams of two ranges, Chayan and Vichayan within self as Azhi. Within the Space Vichaya Thevams, as Thapa ulakam, took over as Aazhi and caused the establishment of An(h) avam (Harmanics) for further activities to a greater extent, causing evolution of Waves of lesser frequencies, mainly Ol(h)i alaikal, the light waves, by Anhavam (Harmonics), which passed through Aazhi. As no mass was existing, the light waves could not manifest itself as well as Aazhi, and this State was termed as "Chudar Aazhi", the Aazhi, which is contained within self.

At this stage Azhi, the fence, (shell), contained Thapa Ulakam of Visuva Thevams (Cosmic Waves), and within which the Space, termed Chudar Aazhi, of Light Waves,

The Azhi is termed at this stage as Vaikuntam. (Vithi- An(h)avam, + Vihitha –various forms and denominations +Kuntam;Vithi+vihitha =Vai+kuntam).

CHAPTER 15

Creation of Vasus (Basic Particles)
(Vasu –Basic Particle):

It is mentioned that eight Vasus, as mentioned below, were created (Vasu - Basic Particle).

1. **Athiyaman**: Ath-Prime own self; +Iyam-function; +An-Prime control. Thus –Prime Control of functions caused by

'Own self' as the Prime one.

Vichaya Thevams (Cosmic Waves of lower Range), evolved in Thapa Ulakam, ventured into the Space (Chudar Aazhi) from all directions and passed through, being induced by the primary Kinetic Energy from the Blue-Black waves.

While passing through, two of the waves met face to face. As both are identical and of the same caliber, they could neither touch each other, nor change their direction, resulting in stoppage/halt. But, since there is continuous dissipation of Kinetic Energy, pressure was built up between the two, resulting in the vivisection of a Miniscule Particle out of Azh. This is the Prime Basic Particle carved out of the Core (Karu), and is termed, "Athiyaman", and, as defined above, is the Prime Control of all functions caused by Own Self as the Prime One.

2) **Anirutthan**: A–Atru, undoing; +niruttha(m)-Stoppage/halt; +n –case ending, indicating the nature of the mass. i.e., 'the one that undid the halt/stoppage of the waves'.

After vivisection, a minute particle from self, as Athiyaman, the pressure continued from outside that particle. As a result/fruition of the pressure, a tiny Particle, smaller than itself, was evolved within Athiyaman. The pressure continued, due to which, this particle was ejected out of Athiyaman. This tiny particle is termed, "Anirutthan'

This was the first mass created in Nature.

This particle moved away at a great velocity from Athiyaman for a little distance, but being controlled by Athiyman, started orbiting around it.

Being a mass, one of the Vichaya waves was attracted by it, resulting in deviation of its path, enabling it to continue its passage. While Anirutthan turned around in its orbit, the other wave was also diverted accordingly.

As this Vasu undid the stoppage of the two Waves, it was named as such.

3. **Sankaran**: Sanka(m) –Associate; +ra- perform/ activity; +n- case ending, indicating its nature.

After the initial cycle of the orbit, Anirutthan could not be alone, and, just as a child clinging to its mother, Anirutthan moved towards Athiyaman and clung to it. This action of association, leading to the formation of third Vasu, was termed, 'Sankaran'.

Athiyaman, being a particle of Karu (core) itself, is defined as 'Eternal'.

Anirutthan being a mass, is destined to perform, and, therefore, defined as 'Time-bound'.

Anirutthan, the mass, is duty-bound, and cannot remain idle as Sankaran, and, therefore is defined "Nilai Atravan, i.e.,'Unstable'.

[Note: Karu (Core of Nature) initiated Kinetic Energy in the form of Waves, by self-priming Pressure within 'Own Self', whereas, in Space, pressure was built from outside by the Waves on 'Own Self' initiating the Creation]

Chudar Aazhi – The Universe in which the Basic Particles are evolved. This Phographic Image is termed "Nebula' in Astro Physics. Random evolution of Basic Particles with the dissipation of Kinetic Energy manifests as Ring. Formation of Neutron Star is in process, which can be seen as the Glowing Globe in the yonder. This wonder of the Astro feat is glorified as, The God's Own Ring'.

These are the ones, mentioned as, 'Proton, Electron and Neutron'. But, these being the initial ones, underwent four more stages of process and established themselves before commencing the Evolution of Nature.

CHAPTER 16

Neutron Star (Sankara Mandalam) and Big Bang (Chitharal)

As narrated in paragraphs above, the process of establishing self as Athiyaman, creation of Anirutthan leading to Sankaran, continued by innumerable cosmic Waves passing through the Space, and at one stage, a massive Mandalam-range of Sankara Vasus was formed. This is what is denoted in present day Science as "**NEUTRON STAR**

Chitharal – "The Big Bang": As Sankaran Vasus being unstable, Athiyaman [Proton-1st stage], the main Vasu in each Sankaran, evolved "Sankara ahkani", in Wave form, around it**'s periphery.**

".Ahkani: Ahk – Prime concept of involvement; an - Prime concept of Control, and, e-enablement. Thus, Enablement of prime concept of involvement under Prime control. This manifests as Patruthal – catch, padarthal-spread, and Seer aathal – neutralize/methodize in seriatum. Fifteen Ahkanis, commencing from Sankara Ahkani, are mentioned of which Fire is one.

Sankara Ahkani Waves are what is denoted as 'Gamma Ray' in present day Science.

The Energy dissipated by this Ahkani, instigated the Aniruttha [Electron-1st Stage] particles and was pushed away with great force. This magnificent Celestial Performance is glorified as the "Big Bang". The dissipation of Energy was massive, spreading light, as though of a festive Fire works, (Chitharal –Scattering).

Big Bang –Sankara Ahani Chitharal.

4) **Kallhazhahkar**: Kallh-fermented lactation from Cocoanut/Palmyra (toddy), bewilderment; +azh-Own self; +ahk - prime involvement, +ar - Prime (concept) performance.

Thus, Prime own-self, is the prime factor of involvement in performance/activities.

Countless Aniruttha Particles, devoid of Energy of its own, remained bewildered, as though inebriated. This Stage was defined as "Kallh Azhahku"- the beautiful sight as though inebriated. In today's science it is called, 'SUPER NOVA'.

Kallazhaku - Super Nova.

Wherever Aniruttha particles (Vasus) were within the Orbital distances, Athiyaman Vasus remained as such, while those, which were away from Orbital distance, were naturalized as 'Azh -the Core'. Such of the Athiyaman Vasus in Kallh azhahku is the third Vasu, viz., Kallh Azhahkar.

5) **Appan**: Ap - Prime concept of Catch hold; +An- Prime Concept of Control – Prime one that holds as the Prime Controller. At this Stage, Athiyaman [1st stage] Vasu, which turned as Kalh Azhahkar in Kallazhahku (Super Nova) primes Chavitha Ahkani around its periphery in Wave form. (Chavitha –pronounced softly as 'savitha').

Chavitha Ahkani – Cha – righteous; v – basis of taking responsibility; Itha – functional character. Thus, the wave taking responsibility for righteous functions/activities. This is defined as, 'Karia sivantha alai". Karia – The one which functions within Karu-core, i.e., infra; sivantha - reddish, i.e., **Infra Red waves/rays**. Also defined as Adippadai Anal Thiran – (Adippadai- Basic-Basis; Anal-Thermo, and Thiran-Kinetic Energy), i.e., Basic Kinetic Energy.

At this stage, Azh as Athiyaman, primed Infra Red Waves around its Periphery, himself forming its Core, remaining himself as though in a cave.

This form of Azh is glorified as 'Kuhan' (kuhai-cave), and also Kovindan: Ko-exalted/supreme; vindan-wonder. And as such it means, 'Supreme Wonder'.

Also referred to as Aathi Appan –Prime stage of Appan, is the fourth stage of Azh.

The 5th Vasu (Basic Particle) 'Appan' turned definitive, which is termed as 'Proton' in present day Science.

(Sanskrit – Purushah).

6) **Virinchi**: (viri - spread and expansively perform; chi-righteously induced). The one being induced to perform righteously.

As Chavitha Thevam passed through, being Basic Kinetic Energy, instigated the Aniruttha particles, due to which, they were awakened from inebriation, and transformed as Virinchi, the 6th Basic Particle. On instigation, Virinchi got four faces, viz., Neel(h)am –length, Akalam - width, Aazham - depth as three faces, and the fourth one being 'Uiyir Patthu kadan- bondage, i.e., as the induced three dimensional functions and bondage as its natural activity.

This is the second stage of Basic particle, termed as 'Electron', in present day Science. (Sanskrit –Brahmah with four faces).

Instigated by Chavitha Thevam (Infra Red Rays), the awakened Virinchi (Electron) particles moved towards the nearby Protons and started circumambulating them, in Parivattoms (Orbits) and thus Atoms (An(h)u) were formed.

As there were lot more electrons, and as they could not be accommodated in one Orbit, they started forming more orbits, one over the other, each one termed as An(h)am (period/Shell). Atoms, Varying from the single shell (an(h) am), i.e. Appu (Hydrogen) and Itha (Helium) onwards were evolved.

7) **Sankaran**. At this stage the Sankaran particle turns definitive, and positioning its as Nalh Nilai –Fulcrum in very many ranges of Atoms. This

one is termed 'Neutron', the third Basic Particle, as mentioned in Present day Science.

With more number of Electrons on outer shells in Atoms with four shells (An(h)ams) and beyond, pressure increased on electrons in the inner shells, resulting in one of the electrons in the first Orbit/Shell slipped inside and clinged to Proton(Appan) forming Sankaran, as the seventh Basic particle. (An(h)am – period/span of time).

CHAPTER 17

Atchini the 8th Basic Particle.

Alh- basis of dimensional limitation +chi-righteous inducement +nh-Basis of time factor, and e-enablement. The one that is the basis and enable measuring limits, and also a factor of time. It is defined as the one that holds light waves as 'Chudar' and splits it when the waves contacted any mass. It can be understood by the terms, 'Photon', the massless particle, and **<u>'spectrum'</u>** as known in science of today.

Ranges of various Light waves (Olhi Alaikal) were evolved from Cosmic Waves on the basis of An(h)avam (Harmonics), the highest being Neelam (blue), from the Cosmic wave (Blue-Black) itself, and Yellow of lesser Range of frequency. And lower still, Red waves. These were blended and entwined together by 'Chudar' such that they could not reveal themselves and remain colourless. This colourless depiction is termed "Ven(h)" and this (Chudar Aazhi) Space is also termed, 'Venh Aazhi'.

This blended Entwinement can be undone and effective to the extent depending on the mass on which the light falls by Konha Alham (angular and dimensional limits).

This effect is termed Atchini, the 8th Vasu (Basic Particle). In today's Science this is termed Spectrum. Atchini is termed as Photon a massless Particle.

With the evolution of Atoms (Anhu) and Spectrum, Evolution of Nature commenced.

CHAPTER 18

Evolution of Nature - Galaxy

Evolution of Nature (Iyarkaiyin Parinamam) is in four stages and termed Naal Vahai Yuhkam.(Sanskrit – Vibhavam – Chatur Yugam)

Yuhkam Yi-(Consonant) Basis of function + uhkam – acceptable in Toto without any ambiguity or doubt.. The word thus means, Basis of acceptable Function. In this context it implies, 'Evolution'.

I. Natchathira Kootam –Galaxy:

1) Macchiyam: M-mass +Ach-Prime concept of righteousness +iyam-function. Thus, functions of all that created within the Space are based on righteousness.

Vinh Meen –Stellar Fish: When looked above the head from North Pole, the Galaxy could be seen in the form of a Fish, with 'Thiruva Star (Pole Star) at the base, and 'Thiru Onam at the nostril tip of it.

[Note: Till recently it was assumed that the Galaxy was serpentine, but during 1991-92, a Professor of Nagoya University charted the stars and found that they were in the form of a 'Cigar'. This discovery only confirms that the findings of Mayans/Chithars long ago, that the Galaxy is in the form of a Fish is true. (Sanskrit- Sisumara Samsthanam –Dolphin Range)]

Thiruva (Pole star), which formed the base, is also a Constellation. While the Sun is at the end of one of the Fins, two other Stars, Apichit and Arunthathi formed the other Fin.

From the Pole, Arunthathi could be seen at half the right angle, i.e. 45 degrees (thithi), and Apichit at an angle, bisecting between Thiruva and Arunthathi, i.e., at 22-1/2 degrees from Thiruva Star. Thus these four Stars form Thiruva Constellation.

Inclination of the Earth assessed as 22-1/2 degrees, was also based on this.

2) Koormam: Next stage of Evolution of Nature after the creation of Fish (Stellar fish). Koora-roof/Shell... Koorma –Natural formation like a shell.

After the evolution of Sun and formation of Earth from it, the Earth consisting of Radio-active particles, underwent various evolutionary processes (Which were detailed earlier under 'Manvanthiram). The Radio-active particles were caught hold by Mukkan(h) Asu (Ozone) and oxidized, reducing them as residuary particles of Metals and non-metals, resulting in reduction of temperature. At one stage Graphite(Mahi) compounded with Asbestos Kalnaar) formed Mahithalam, over which, the metals turned from vapour to molten-fluid form, settled down as solid crusts, forming Layers of Plates (Thalaa thalam)on the Earth. This formation is termed, Koormam.

3) Varahkam: - Rhinosaurus.

When temperature fell down considerably, Waters too formed with Appu (hydrogen) interacting with Irukan-Asu (Bivalent Oxygen). Water too turned liquid later, and the Dusts of various metal/non metal compounds fell on the Layers of Plates, along with water, with a force similar to that of the Charge of Rhinosaurus.

4) **Ari**: -Lion. (Sanskrit word, Hari, is a Phonetic variant of Thamizh word, the other one being,'Nrusimham').

During the process of formation of Layers of Plates, various gases were captivated below and in between these Layers. On cooling further, the Plates shrunk considerably, building high pressure of gases. At one stage the gases tore the Plates and escaped into atmosphere. This resulted in Plates moving with great noise, resembling that of a lion's roar. Wherever the plates moved away deep pits formed, wherein water flowed in forming seas and lakes, and wherever they dashed against each other, rocks and mud raised above, forming hills and mountains. This lead to flowing of rivers, evolving the Earth conducive to life system. This phenomenon of Nature was termed 'Ari'.

[Note: 1) Due to the activities of Seismic lines formed in 'Irasa Thalam' below the Plates/Mahithalam strata, several metals on the Plates melted and started flowing like rivers of lava, which frequently erupted, forming Volcanoes. Two such volcanoes formed at both the Poles (Vata-North and Then-South munais-Poles). Over a long period of time the Volcano at the North Pole erupted massively, resulting in burst and submersion of this Volcano. Thereafter, Arctic Ocean was formed [Paarkadal in Thamizh]. The one at Southern Pole cooled down and became inactive. These two Poles were cooled down considerably because of seasonal variations, and Arctic Ocean froze. Southern landscape surrounding the Pole, what is called Aati Theevu (Antarctic), was also frozen, and ice formed on it.

2) When the volcano at the North pole erupted, obnoxious gases, including Aalakaalam (fluorine Gas) came out and spread over the Earth. Calcium metal (Kambu ulokam-Thamizh), calcinated because of the rise in temperature, readily absorbed the Fluorine, forming White Clay.]

At this stage, earth, mainly within the two Iraasis (Lines of Cancer and Capricorn), Lime stones (Ota kal), and dust containing the oxides of various metals, mainly Iron (Aiyan), noble metal-Gold (Pon) and silver (velli), formed the earth. Water, obtained from melting of ice, started flowing as rivers. As practically all the oxygen were bi-valent and remained as oxides of metals and water, the sky was clear with other gases, and water vapour.. When Sun rose, the light from it, due to radio-active rays, chief of them being Ultra violet Rays (Karia Sivantha Neela kathirveechu: Karia Sivantha –Infra Red; Neela –Blue colour rays –seemingly violet), spread on the earth As Asu was bivalent, it was active, and therefore, the oxides of metals turned Radio-Active releasing Oxygen. Calcium metal had great affinity or Ultra Violet Rays, and they absorbed these Rays and in this process, temperature raised very high and Calcium rocks and stones, released Carbon Dioxide (Kari AmilaVaayu) into atmosphere forming Quick Lime (Calcium Oxide).

After Sunset, the atmosphere cooled down and water vapour in atmosphere formed clouds, leading to heavy rains.. Carbon dioxide gas dissolved in the rain and the atmosphere was cleared of it. The Quicklime reacted to water and formed Lime Water (Ota Neer - Calcium Hydroxide), releasing (Mukkan Asu Nascent Oxygen- Ozone. Ozone, thus released, rose above the Sky and formed the Ozone Layer.

The next morning at Sunrise, the Ultra Violet Rays passed from the Sun was split by the Ozone Layer. While Blue Colour Rays spread along the Ozone Layer, the Infra Red Rays (Karia Sivantha Alai) pierced through the Layer and reached the Earth, as Basic Thermal Energy, transforming the Earth conducive for evolution of Life System.

CHAPTER 19

Evolution of Life System

This evolution is also in four stages, termed, 'Naal Vahkai Yuhkam'. (Sanskrit – Vibhava Avatharam- Chatur Yugam). -

1) The four stages of evolution of Life System are as follows:

1) Viyarvayil uyirthal – sprouting from dampness,
2) Vithayil Uyirthal – Sprouting from seeds,
3) Muttaiyil uyirthal - hatched from eggs, and
4) Karuvil Uyirthal - Birth from womb.

While the first two lead to the initial stages of evolution as Algae and Fungus/mushrooms, which formed the primary stages of stationary live systems, i.e., Plants, vines, trees, etc., the later two lead to the evolution of moving lives, viz., flying creatures and birds and moving lives, worms, reptiles, animals and humans.

Uyir: uy—Basis of self priming function + ir-basis of natural activity. i.e., Basis of self priming function as a natural activity, which can be termed as Germination as a self priming function by nature.

The germination is in varieties depending on place and climatic conditions, and termed, 'Itchavaahu': It - place as basis; vaahu- varying systems, based on the place.

In Sanskrit – Ikshvaku, phonetic variant of Thamizh nomenclature, which is explained thus: Itch is the phonetic expression of Sneeze, i.e., germination out of dampness.

It was already narrated under Manvanthira period, at the seventh stage of the evolution of Earth. After the dust in the atmosphere fell on the Earth along with water, the sky became clear, and the land was slushy. Algae germinated and the whole Earth looked green and beautiful. Then thin and small variety of bamboos sprouted, and then termites from which the moving life was also evolved.

The above was evolved initially at the fag end of the 3rd stage of the Evolution of Nature –Varaham.

After the mountains and seas were formed on the Earth, the evolution system commenced again, as algae, and on mountain slopes as fungus/mushrooms.

As ice was formed on the peaks of mountains water table started receding, life system also had to adapt to the changes. Due to this, the plants were evolved with root-bulbs (Kizhanku, example- Potato, beet root, etc.) from which the plants sprouted and spread. Plantain trees, which retains water in its trunks were evolved.

Though the above species flowered, and plantains bore fruits, they did not have seeds with germinating capability.

Later, cactus (Thaazhai) which retains water in its leaves, and can sustain dry climatic conditions were also evolved. Of the various species of Cactus, included Poo thaazhai with fragrant flowers (in South India). The cactus also grew tall in ancient times from which evolved, cocoanut, Palmyra, Betel nut, Dates and Palm trees, each conducive to the soil and temperature conditions prevailing in different areas. Of these, Cocoanut, referred to as 'Rathitharan', was considered holy in India, as twice born, as the plant germinated within the Nut-fruit and sprouted out, and later, fell on earth and grew as tree. As brahmans were declared twice-born, the cocoanut was considered on par with Brahmans, the holy ones, and it is offered to Deities.

Because of seasonal variations, Nunn(h)uyir* kirumi(micro organisms), which causes uyirthal (Germination of life), started protecting themselves by forming a shell on its own, remained on earth, and sprouted, when it rained. Thus cereals and plants bearing seeds were also evolved.

(*Nunnuyir – nunn(h) to be pronounced as in 'put')

There is one unique tree in India, called 'Banyan Tree'.

Grass varieties known as Elephant grass grew in this Country. Due to vagaries of Nature, a variety of this grass adapted itself as tree with branches, from which clusters of roots grew, like beard, downwards, embedded into earth forming another tree, and by this process, it grew as a massive cluster of trees, covering large areas, running to several square miles. Though this tree bore fruits, the seeds did not have Chromosomes, and therefore, could not germinate.

Then Arasa Maram - Peepal Tree, a species of the Banyan

Tree, but did not grow roots from is branches, was evolved by Nature. This grew tall, spreading into sky. This is a Rain Tree. This has various medicinal properties. As Such, it is called Arasa - the king. It bore fruits, and unlike the Banyan, this species sprouts from these seeds.

Its seeds have a very important medicinal property. These seeds are processed by Chittha (Siddha) physicians and administered to those women, who could not conceive. This, as a herb, strengthens the Ova and increases the Chromosomes in women, enabling conception.

Now let us take up the 3rd, Birth from eggs and 4th, birth from womb (sapiens).

Alongside, egg-laying termites evolved from the rotten leaves and twigs that fell on the slushy earth. These built water-proof Termite hills and thereby, earth also methodically hardened. When it rained water entered the hills, they grew wings on their own, flew out of the pits for survival.

Then onwards flying creatures, viz., Bees, Wasps, etc., and thereafter birds of different species were also evolved.

Further, crawling ones were evolved, as detailed below:

1) <u>Chapari</u> (Pronounced also as Sapari) (Sanskrit –Mathsya Avatharam). Cha – Righteous + pari- pervading. This defines the character of the Fish. This was evolved in Ponds, rivers, and later in Sea, evolved different species, leading to the evolution of Mammals, viz., Shark, Dolphins and Whales, which conceived in the womb and gave birth to their siblings.. (In ancient days Seas were like wide rivers only.)

(At first, micro organisms in water built a physic as their abode. Even now these are existing in Bay of Bengal and are called Matchiyam. They do not have teeth, huge, and while they take water inside for breathing, micro organisms entered in as their abode and grew.)

It is said that the fish knew nothing but affinity, grew in thousands. Vagaries of Nature, though destructive, really enabled the evolution of different species. By this process of Nature both egg-laying and the one that gave birth by conception in their womb were evolved from water/ sea.

CHAPTER 20

Evolution of life system in other areas of the Eastern Hemisphere:

First reptile species, that breath in air, was also evolved in Water, viz., Crocodiles. They were called. Makaram Ma-keeping the mouth open while on the banks, as though expressing 'ma', and later as Muthalai – muthal- the first one that can breath in air, and also first of the reptile species. It is carnivorous and egg-laying species, as other reptiles too. In ancient times, the Crocodiles in Makara Theevu – Australia, were so huge, that they dragged the elephants, which came for drinking water, killed and ate them. In the course of time whole Elephants species was eliminated/liberated in that island. Even today in India this is elaborately narrated as 'Gajendra Moksham' (Gajendra – Elephant species; Moksham –liberation).

'Thar' Desert in Rajasthan was a Pure Water Sea in ancient times. It was so vast that it extended up to Southern Iran (Persia). Ice on the Imaiya Kootam (Himalayan Range), as it is called today) melted and spilled over to form this Sea, and as such, was called 'Chinthu'. Chinthu (Thamizh) means spill over. (It was later called 'Sindhu ', a phonetic variant of Thamizh nomenclature. This has nothing to do with Indus and India which were coined out by migrants out of their imagination, devoid of historical sanctions.). It was surrounded by dense forest, such that even hand could not move in. Several waterborne vines, such as Chenthamarai-Lotus, Alli-lily, Kuvalhai –Blue Lotus, were spread over in it. Several species of Fish, and also birds, living on this fish were also mentioned. Here, the first of the reptile species, viz., Earth-Worm was evolved, which ploughed through the earth and lived. Moreover it was termed Eela – bisexual living being. Several other bisexual species, centipedes, and insects like cockroaches, spiders scorpions, crabs, etc. also evolved.

It was also mentioned, that, when man started to acquire knowledge, first thing he did was denuding the forest. After denudation during the course of time, Top Soil was blown away by the West Wind, and only a small part of it is left today, called 'Pushkaram' near Ajmir (Rajasthan).

South of the above Sea was Katcha Nilam, today known as Kutch. Kutcha in Thamizh means, 'Crude and not developed'. The name by itself explains the condition of the land. It was generally marshy, full of quagmires, that any reptile or worm species moved in this land were buried in them.. Only shrubs grew. Worms of various species evolved from the rotten leaves and twigs. The main life evolved was snail. It was Jell-like and built Shells as their abode, and carried them on their back wherever they moved. They lived on the worms in the slush and reptiles caught in quagmires. Many portions of this landscape, were submerged into Sea because of natural vagaries, including catastrophes. (Snail was mentioned in Sanskrit as 'Maha Bali, meaning, great strength'.

In Central Asia, what is known today as Gobi Desert and Mongolia, including Northern China were called 'Eelaa Veli'. The very name indicates that it is the Land of Reptiles, Earth Worms to start with. Being bisexual they were, a time came, when some of the species became aggressive and dominant, over the weaker ones, leading to evolution of male and female genders in the reptile species as snakes. During the Course of time, evolved from the same species, huge ones, egg laying and then mammals of the same species.

2) Koormam: (Tortoise) When water table reduced on the Earth, huge tortoises egg-laying, were evolved, which could live both in Water and Land. This species is also considered to be evolved from Snails. They not only lived in Sea, but also in deep and perennial rivers. They had huge shells (Koora- Roof/

shelter) on their backs they could draw the head and legs into the shells to protect themselves.

3) <u>Varaahkam</u>: In the course of time leading to change of landscapes and seasonal variations, the tortoises started to move in high rise lands and live on grass and roots. On this, their heads and legs stabilized and evolved an animal and a mammal. The hard shell over its back also was transformed as thick skin. This one was termed <u>Varaahkam-Rhinoceros.</u> Having been earth borne, this animal had developed five senses, look, hear, smell, make sounds, and feeling by physical contact. Because of this caliber, and being the first of animal species, is also called Kaandava Vilangu.

Kaandava: ka –the physic, the one that performs for living, +aanda - Rule/control,+ va- Vahkam, i.e., taking responsibity. Vilanku - animal. Thus, Kaandavan is the one that controls the physical activities of the animal through senses. This is Static Electricity, generated in the glands as well as in muscular movements. This electricity triggers the nerves, which carry it to the Reverberatory Cells of the Brain.

From Rhinosaurus, evolved bear, which had strong legs and could stand up and walk on hind legs, and climb trees also. It could use the front legs as hands. On this evolution, thick skin got split up as cluster of hair. These had a high sense of smelling, and it is said that they could smell and identify any object from a distance of two to three kilometers, depending on the direction of the wind. They are vegetarian, but eat fish also.

From Rhinosaurus evolved wild Boars, almost akin to the former., then pigs, porcupines, etc..

4) <u>Chataari</u>: In evolution of Nature the fourth one being Ari, akin to the characteristic of a lion. In the evolution of life-system the nomenclature, Chatari refers to the Lion itself. Chatam –frame, here marking the borders

of the landscape, within which it rules and lives; +ari —enablement of Prime concept of performance.

(In Psychology (Thamizh) this nomenclature also refers to the first twenty pairs of Chromosomes of both male and female sparmatosa.)

From the bears evolved Apes and monkeys, etc., according From the bears evolved Apes and monkeys, etc., according to the habitats and availability of food.

For the same reasons carnivorous animals, as ferocious as Shark in Sea, and as powerful and noble as Whales and Dolphins were also evolved consisting mainly of two categories, the Cat(Tiger) and the Dog(lion) families, respectively.

As a prelude to the evolution of human species, the bear and then ape were evolved from Rhinoceros.

In tropical forests honey was the favourite food for the bears. The taste of honey dripped from the honeycombs attracted them towards it. They were individualistic and led lonely life. Their wants were limited and spent most of the time in sleep/slumber in caves reclining on their backs. Though eye sight was fairly good, they depended on smelling for identification.

When apes were evolved, they had good eye sight and started observing and identified. This enabled the evolution of the Ape Man. The sight enabled their identification efficacy, leading to community life. This observation also lead to acquiring knowledge basically each one building the capability of activities, and during the course of years the first human was evolved.

The evolution of life system up to Chatari is mentioned as the first Yuhkam of four stages, viz., Fish (Chapari), Tortoise (Koormam), Rhinoceros (Varaahkam) and Chataari (lion). Among various species of Animals only Lion was chiefly mentioned, because of its magnanimity, living as a family of husband-wife and children. While the male one protected its family, the female one hunts, allowed the male-head as the first one to take its share, then its cubs, and finally it took its share. It also allowed other smaller carnivorous animals and birds to eat the left over's. They never ate the ones hunted by other animals, and never saved the remnants of the hunted one for later consumption, as tigers do. This was the reason why the pack is called, "the Pride of lion". The man has learnt a lot from the traits of the lion to lead a family life, and especially the chieftains/the kings, to take responsibilities as Rulers.

CHAPTER 21

Evolution of Human.

Three Stages The next one is the first three stages of Human evolution, denoted as **'Mupparinama Yuhkam'**, i.e., "Three stages of Human Evolution", which are as follows:

1) **Vaamanan**: Vaa - Vaay– Mouth, here it is interpreted as Speech; mana(m) –Mind, i.e., capability of thinking and remembering. First of the human species evolved from the Ape-Man who started standing erect and walked, using the front legs as hands. This enabled him to become independent of the Control of Nature, thereby he could observe the Nature's activities and exploit them to his advantage. The caliber of the man was depicted in the form of a metaphorical story, thus:

"A five year old boy, initiated as a student, approached the King Maavali (Sanskrit-Mahabali) and sought for three steps of land to be measured by his own foot. The king was surprised at this request and wondered as to how much land he could measure with his tiny foot, and readily granted. Then, the boy measured the earth with one step, measured the space with his second step, and finding no place for his third step, asked the king to provide for the third. The king sat and bowed down asking the boy to set his third step on his head. Accordingly the boy set his third foot on the King's head and pressed him hard and sent him to Mahithalam, the base of Plates within the Earth."

In the above story, the king is the Nature that controls the Earth, and Maavali – meaning the one with massive strength, i.e., the Earth itself. The story thus reveals that the Nature that controls the Earth, granted all its possessions to the tiny man, who took over all that Nature had provided by the skill of the knowledge he acquired from within self. This showed the evolution of the Man with great skills, acquired through his knowledge, can measure the world, the space and, of course, gain knowledge about the strata in the depth of the earth. As a first step of the knowledge, he keenly observed and developed his skills by acting with his physic, mainly his hands. Thus, the knowledge was evolved from 'than - thiram'. Than-'Of Self'; thiram- Capability(to act), i.e., Technic.

['than '– pronounced as in 'that']

The Man, with "Anpu" (Innocence) as the basis of mind, started living as a community near water sources, with the skillful and strong man as the leader. While females, children and old people stayed in the settlement, adult males, along with adolescent boys of above 12 years of age moved out to collect food and other ingredients for livelihood. They started to build long sheds with grass and twigs to protect themselves from Sun and rain. To protect themselves from wild animals some of them trained themselves in fighting skills with sticks and logs, and stood guarding the settlement. The one acquired skilled in eking out was called, 'Varan', i.e., 'the one who has taken responsibility to act'

Vari (portion paid by the Varan) –Tax/Tribute: On return from work the men took a portion of what they colleted for themselves and offered the balance to the chieftain. He took a portion for himself and apportioned the rest among the inmates.

They observed that forest fire lit up the sky at night and also gave warmth and excessive heat. After fire, they strayed into the forest and found the burnt/roasted plants, fruits and even the flesh of animals tasted differently and also soft. He also saw animals ran away when forest was gutted. Finding out that when the wind blew dry grass and twigs, especially bamboos rubbed, by which fire was lit. Based on this knowledge he tried and succeeded in lighting fire. Initially he used fire for keeping the wild animals away, but later various duties were evolved with fire as the fuel.

With development of activities, he turned various voices into single syllables and then words, primarily to direct the method and later the evolution of knowledge into language, viz, teaching and training.

Then building relationship and family life commenced and having huts as homes and also had a fire place in each home. Alongside he removed gravels and tilled the land with the horns of dead animals and twigs/sticks broken from trees, and sowed seeds during rainy seasons and thus the first and prime culture, i.e., Agriculture (Akara kalai) commenced. He found the sharp edge of stones could cut, started using the stones as tools. When the Lava from volcanoes cooled, finding shining and tough objects in it, he analysed and segregated such of the metals, that he could. From this primarily Iron (Ayan-Thamizh, The one obtained as the prime one) came into the culture. Following this copper came in later. The people who became experts were glorified as Mayans. Two separate cultures emanated, namely, karumaar, Blacksmiths and Iympon (five non-ferrous metals, copper - chembu, silver - velli, gold - pon, Tin-kalaayam and zinc- narakam). Then pursuit of knowledge continued out of aptitude and analysis, and developed knowledge in different branches. It is mentioned on Thamizh Ancient History that there were 64 Aaya kalais i.e., Treatises in the past.

[Several of them are still preserved and practiced devoutly by several experts, though not recognized and are now socially depressed classes. This has reached such a stage that Mayan is derided by migrants to the extent of terming him as a 'demon' - 'Mayaasura'.].

Educational system was initiated with four main paths: 1) Vitthai –Vitthu –seed, i.e., knowledge that sprouts from within. Vitthai indicates the process based on the aptitude of Children. 2) Thaanam – tha -Theism, and anam- subservience as prime one. The word implies that both the teacher and the taught should be subservient to the knowledge as the Prime one. 3) Thapam – Tha-theism, pa-to hold, pursuit in the path of knowledge 4) Sathiyam- mentally be straightforward to the knowledge gained, i.e., righteous in action/performance based on knowledge gained. Thereafter, they codified the social way of life with four stages, viz., 1) pati- Education, 2) Nilai -Steadfast in life based on the education, 3) Idai -Retirement from active participation in domestic and professional activities, and, 4) Veedu- Completely delink from social and sensual relationships and to attain serenity, thus prepare for the eventual end. This also was codified into four serial concepts of mental agility, viz., 1) Aram-Self control and social amicability, 2) Porul – wealth, to eke out life by performing one's duties, 3) Kaamam- taking a Partner as life companion, and, 4) leave away all the worldly possessions to one's lineage, delinking from worldly relationships, and remain with universal thoughts till the release of life bondage.

Even about 7,500 years ago people were righteous and secular without pride or prejudice in the Northern part, and the people in the South continued to be righteous up to 2nd A.D., till various sects from Mongol areas and the middle east, mainly what is today called Afganisthan, and Central Asia, migrated.

2) <u>Parasu Rama</u>: He was born as the tenth son of Jamadagni, Brahman, and Renuka devi(Mother), who were living at 'Mahisha Sthali, i.e., Land of Buffaloes, which was South of today's Iran, and southwest of Sinthu (Sind in today's Pakistan).

These were constructed about 7,500 years ago. In ancient times, this landscape (marshy lands) was called Mahisha Sthali, i.e., Land of Buffeloes'. These buildings were constructed with Lime Stones, such that they could withstand Tides. This was the place were Parasurama was born as tenth son of Jamadagni.[Population was very low during the period of Parasurama and the cities came up long time, i.e., after development of civilisation.]

Jamadagni named him "Rama', but as there was three of the same name, historically glorious, he was identified with Parasu-Plough Yoke his weapon, and was prefixed to his name and became to be known as 'Parasu Rama'.

Mahishasthali, i.e., Land of Buffallows (Marshy landscape) was south of the place is called, 'Pahman', phonetic variant of 'Bahman' which again is a phonetic variant of 'Brahman'. The lineages of Jamadagni clan are now known as Dutta/Dutt. According to their Legendry, 'Once the three Gods, Brahma, Vishnu and Shiva, wishing to test the 'Chastity of Anusuya, wife of Athri, went to her abode disguising themselves as Brahmans, and asked for Alms. When Anusya came out to serve alms, they asked her to come nude and serve.. She, by the power of her chastity, transformed them into a child and fed them from her breast. This child is God Duttathreya, and the faithful Dog (shuva) was his career of his glory (vahana).

Mahishasthali was part of 'Kusa Dweepa –the land of Greenery, consisting the Plains of Afghanistan, Iran, Iraq and Syria. There were many 'Kshatriya kings, ruling in this Land, and Arjuna, popularly known as 'Kaartha veeriya Arjuna' was the King off all other Kings, whom all other kings obeyed and paid Tributes. As he was a Kshatriya, he could punish others and none else could punish him. Brahmins supported the Kshatriyas. As such, he led a licentious life, usurped many women, through whom he begot thousand sons, who formed his Army.

Jamadagni was rearing a milking she-buffalo and named it 'Kamadenu'. Once King Arjuna visited his abode. Finding Kamadenu and tasting its milk, took it away much ignoring the pleadings of Jamadagni. Parasu Rama was not present at that time, and the other nine sons were mute, watching the incident. When Parasu Rama returned home, he heard of the incident and got wild with anger. He took a Plough-Yoke as his weapon and reached Arjuna's Residence. When Arjuna's sons resisted, he killed them all including the King Arjuna, and brought back the buffalo. In the melee one of Arjuna's son escaped, biding time to avenge his father's death.. On one day, when Parasu Rama was away, the son of late King Arjuna, killed Jamadagni and ran away. When Parasu Rama returned, he became furious, took the Owe to annihilate the licentious Kshatriyas. Very many kings in the Middle East were killed and, on hearing his arrival, many others ran away into hiding.

Thus, people were relieved of the atrocities of Kshatriyas and he became a legendary Personality. The people considered him the God incarnate as 'he spoke less and fought against atrocities perpetrated on common People'. There is an ancient township in Palestine called "Ramallah", in his glory. Several kings of Salmali (Egypt) were named 'Rameses'. The Capital of Yavana's was named Roma, in his memory. This city is now called 'Rome', and the people were denoted as Romans. Gypsies worship him as 'Romulus', phonetic variant of Ram Allah, as their God.

The landscape of Kusadweepa, were he was born, was carved out and named after him as 'Persia' (phonetic variant of Parasu). Later, as a country, it is now called, Iran.

Late Harry Millar, famous historian and popular writer on various social subjects, wrote an Article in "Indian Express", news paper, some decades ago, brief contents of which are furnished below:

"The Tribal Leaders of North/North West Pakistan used to meet periodically to discuss on various matters of common interest and also to sort out issues, if any, arising among them. If at any time words went out of control and emotions upsurged, such that a fight might break out, an elderly man would get up and declare, "Ram, Ram". On hearing this, the Tribal leaders would calm down and disperse silently. No one was able to explain who this Ram was." Though (Parasu) Rama's history is forgotten in the Middle East and West, his glory is epitomized as above.

His period was about 7,500 years ago. At his old age, he entered Thiruvidam-India, went to Mithila during Rama's (Ayodhya) marriage, blessed him, retired to "Bhadrashravam", on the eastern Bank of Godavari River, and spent the remaining period of his life fixing his mind in 'Shriman Narayana'. In memory of him, this place was also referred to as "Panchavati, where Lord Rama of Ayodhya spent 12 years of his 14-year exile. His historical part is elaborated in 8th (Soma Sects) and 9th (Dravida Sects) Cantos of Shrimad Bhagavatham.

[Bhadrashravam – (Bhadra- protection) secure place to live. This place is now called, "Bhadrachalam" in Khammam District, Andhra Pradesh.

3) **Lord Sri Rama:** The third and equally important in human evolution is the biography of Rama.

It is narrated in 9th Canto of Shrimad Bhagavatham that this India as Thiruvidam (Dravidam in Sanskrit) was the abode of Shudra Race. They were ancient and lived on what they earned by performing their duties. They never accepted anything as gratis/alms from others. They had great aptitude for learning and training. Shudras practiced Sanaathana (Thamizh) code of life. They were referred to as Sanaathanis in Thamizh.

(This race had nothing to do with Varnashrama of Manusmriti, included by the migrants, viz., Yakshas from Middle East, and Rakshas from Mongolian areas).

Some important historical notes based on the 9th Canto of Srimad Bagavatham, as a prelude to Rama's biographical narration, are furnished below to emphasize the greatness of this ancient Dynasty.

1) About 8,300 years ago, Sowdasa, King of Ayodya, on the bank of Sarayu River (U.P.), an ancestor of Rama, started the Game, Aksha Hridam (to observe and decide the movements mentally), which is now known as Chess, for devising strategies in War front. The components then were, the King, Army Chief, Archers and Infantry.

Nala, a Soma Vamshi, who was to capture horses for sacrifice to propitiate Gods, finding them to be friendly, trained them and he himself practiced horse mounting and riding. He befriended Sowdasa and trained him in horse-riding, and in return, learnt the Aksha Hrida game and became a warrior. After this, horses were captured and trained for travelling and hunting game (a pro-war training), and in wars. As horses were no more available for sacrifice, the Yakshas got wild and started propagating false stories against Nala and linking atrociously with Dhamayanthi, wife of Sowdasa and that he suffered by the curse of Sani(Satan). These stories are still in vogue in the name of religion.

Sowdasa was the first to locate Mongolian Rakshasas-Cannibals hiding in the forests on the slopes of Imaiya (Himalaya) Range and killed them. This enraged the Rakshas, who entertained animosity against Ayodya kings and started propagating later, after they also infiltrated and settled down as Kapalika-Sanyasis in Kosala and Magada kingdoms that Sowdasa himself practiced cannibalism. (Buddha mentioned about them to Magada King Ajatasatru, that the Brahman Sanyasis, who performed 'Lohita Homa with Human Blood -500 B.C. – Samajya Pala Sutta).

Later, King Sagara was noteworthy. He strengthened the borders, located the Black nomads, got their heads, mustache and beards neatly shaven and drove them as well as Rakshas far away such that they could not return.

Some Yaksha Brahmins approached him and on their advice started preparations for Horse Sacrifice as 'Ashwa medha Yaga' to propitiate the Gods. But on the advice of Arava Muni (aravam - ancient Thamizh; Arava Muni-Thamizh Scholar), gave up Horse Sacrifice. Annoyed by this, the Brahmins started propagating ill-conceived false stories about him, stating that he had hundred sons, who went in search of the missing king's horse and finding it grazing near Kapila's place, got angry at Kapila mistaking him to have stolen it, and were about to kill. Kapila looked at them with fiery eyes resulting in their being reduced to ashes, and even declared Chitthar Kapila was a Cow. These are continued till date in the name of devotion, practically burying the true History, narrated to King Pareekshit by Sukha and documented in 9th Canto.

Sagara had a son, named, 'Asamanchan', who was well versed in hypnotism and Magic tricks. He pleased the people of Ayodya, very often, by his Magic Tricks. One day he took the children away to Sarayu River and, while people were watching, he threw them, one by one, into the River. The people were shocked, ran to the King and reported the matter. The king was equally shocked, rushed to the place of incident and banished Asamanchan from the Kingdom. Asamanchan felt sorry that people did not understand his action was a Magic, went to the River, brought back the children and handed over to the respective parents. Stating that the King's orders could not be reversed, he left the Kingdom. King felt sorry that he passed order without proper enquiry.

Amsuman, son of Asamanchan, was devoted to his grand father, King Sagara.

Kapila Theertha, where Chitthar Kapilar, the enlightened, spent his last days teaching and spreading knowledge among those who approached him, (About 10,000 years ago) is on the shore of the Sea, about 120 K.M.s south of Kolkatha /Calcutta in West Bengal).

Once Amsuman went on a pilgrimage to Kapila Theertha and found that pilgrims visiting there were suffering without water. Then he dug a river branch from Kaliya River later known as Yamuna River. As this water was meagre, he proceeded to augment from Imaiya Range (known today as Himalaya) but he died before he could take up the work. Bhagiratha, his son and great grandson of Sagara, continued his father's mission, went up the Mountain Ranges, linked the rivulets, formed by molten Ice, dug a River and linked it to Kaliya River. As the water did not flow into the river, he went back the route and found that the water was flowing into a Gorge. He diverted the course and succeeded in bringing copious water. This river dug by him was named, **"Kankai"**, and later called, 'Ganga', a phonetic variant of Thamizh name 'Kankai'. The Milky Way in the Stellar Galaxy was termed **"Akaaya Kankai"**, and the new river was glorified as the one brought from the heavenly space.

But, honouring Bhagiratha, part of this River flowing through West Bengal was named "Bhagirathi" River, i.e., the one born to King Bhagiratha.

This Dynasty was referred to as 'Itamsaarvahu' in Tamizh, i.e., 'sprouting of life system as Algae/Fungus, conducive to the place. In Sanskrit it was mentioned as Ikshvaku kulam, which carries the same meaning. This is only to indicate the antiquity. This Dynasty was also called as 'Raghu kulam'. Raghu refers to the Sun. As the kings of this Dynasty brightened the life of people, they were referred to as such.

Several kings (of the same lineage) later to Bhagiratha, Dasaratha became the King of Ayodhya. He was the first to tether horses to Ratha, i.e., Chariot, and trained himself in the Art of fighting from the Chariot (Charioteer). 'Dasaratha' is the name of Honour. ('Dasa' refers to ten in Arithmetic and also denotes regularisation. His period was about 7,500 years ago, same period of Parasu Rama).

He first married Kowsalya, the princess of Kosala Kngdom. As she could not conceive, he married Kaikeyee, the Princess of Kekaya Kingdom (Ancient name of Nepal). As she also could not conceive, he married Sumithra from a Commoner's family. Even she did not conceive. By then he was 60 year old. Vasishta, The Acharya (enligtened) of Raghu Kula, got a concocttion made out of *Peepal tree seeds, mixed with milk and rice, and gave it to Dasaratha. The King gave it to the queens, and thereafter, they conceived. Kousalya gave birth to Rama, Kaikayee, Bharatha, and Sumithra, the twins, Lakshmana and Shatrugna. On mother's advice, Lakshmana accompanied Rama, while Shatrugna accompanied Bharatha. All of them got educated and trained in warfare, especially Archery. All the four completed their education and training and returned to Ayodya at the age of sixteen.

[*Note: In Ramayana Valmiki refers to the tree as 'Rishya Sringa. Rishya is the phonetic variant of Thamizh nomenclature 'Arasa'tree, and sringa-branches, i.e., tree. Sanskrit nomenclature is Pipiliya vruksha).

Rama was glorified as 'Raghu Kula Thilaka', i.e., The Jewel of Raghu Kula.

Kamban (Pen Name), King of Thiru Azhundur in Tamil Nadu, (7th Century A.D.) in his Epic, "Erama Kaathai" (Biography of Rama), refers to him 'Annal', the 'one who leads all on the righteous path of Life'. He saw the greatness of Rama's life through about 600 couplets of 'Thirukkural', Thamizh Epic, emphasising the Codes of Righteous Life, rendered by Thiruvalluvar.

Kunrathu Ramanusan of the same 7th Century A.D., glorified as the Father of Malayalam Language, authored "Ramayanam Kili Pattu" as the first Epic of that Language, wherein he included the greatness of Rama's Rule as narrated by Suka in 9th Canto of Srimad Bhagavatham.

(Kili – Parrot; Pattu – song. Suka was glorified as Parrot in the sense that whatever he wrote in Maha Bharatha as dictated by Vyasa, and wrote and narrated the 18 Cantos of Srimad Bhagavatham, were true and neither twisted nor included his schisms, like a Parrot, which repeats what it heard or taught).

Rama's biography written by Valmiki is universally known. Every step in Rama's life set the Moral and Righteous path to follow. Rama took all that he learnt from Vasishta, to his heart as Code of Life, and followed himself without deviation.

When Rama completed twenty one years of age, Dasaratha (82 years) decided to declare Rama as the Crown Prince. At that time Bharatha, son of Kaikeyee, his second wife, was away at Kekaya kingdom (Nepal), i.e., his maternal uncle's place. When Manthara, personal attendant of Kaikeyee, heard this, she could not tolerate, and wanted her queen's son, Bharatha, should rule. She conveyed this to Kaikeyee in such a way as to kindle her motherly passion. The evil had started haunting her mind. She, as advised by Manthara, felt that, 'people of Ayodya would not accept her son's rule, if Rama stayed in Ayodya, and, therefore, decided to demand for Rama's exile also.

When Dasaratha went to her apartment to convey his decision, she asked him to grant her two wishes. Without knowing her mental disposition he readily agreed, upon which she demanded that, 1) her son, Bharatha to rule Ayodya, and 2) Rama to live in exile in forest for 14 Years. Dasaratha was shocked, and pleaded to withdraw her second wish on Rama's exile. As she did not yield, he fell unconscious. Then Kaikeyee sent for Rama to whom she conveyed the two wishes granted to her by Dasaratha.

Rama took upon himself, as a son, it was his duty to honour his father's words and left Ayodya, discarding the ornaments and paraphernalia of a Prince. Wearing simple dress as a commoner, and 'Pathuka', (wooden footwear), he set on his journey to forest. His wife, Seetha, could not see herself different from her husband, followed him. His brother Lakshmana too discarded all the princely paraphernalia and accompanied Rama.

Bharatha returned to Ayodya. When his mother informed of the two wishes granted by his father, he refused to take over as King and declared that Rama, being the eldest, was the right person to Rule. He left the palace and met Rama on the bank of River Ganga and pleaded to him not to honour the immoral grants and requested him to return and take over as King.

Rama advised that as Dasaratha's sons. It is their duty to honour the words already granted, and not to look into the morality or consequences.

Bharatha took this advice in true spirit, requested and received Rama's two Pathukas (wooden footwear) and returned. Taking the vow that he would enter Ayodya only with Rama on his return from forest, he stayed at Nandhi Grama (Pleasure village), away from Ayodya, placed Rama's Pathuka on a throne, and ruled on behalf of Rama. He too discarded Royal ornaments and paraphernalia and led a commoner's life. Sathrugna, the fourth brother, also stayed with Bharatha.

Such was the greatness of righteous traits of this Royal family and the people, lived about 7,500 years ago.

Rama, along with his wife and Lakshmana, crossed the river Ganga. On reaching the other bank, the boatman, Guhan stood at a distance from Rama, 'the Prince'. Noticing this, Rama addressed him, "Guha, from now on, we are five brothers including you. Come and embrace me".

This trait of Rama revealed his kinship considring all humans as equals.

From there they reached Bhadrashrava on the bank of Godhavari River, in Dandaka Aaranya (forest). This is the place, where Parasu Rama spent his last days. There he provided a small platform with twigs and a thatched roof on the branch of a tree for Seetha to take rest and sleep. (mentioned as parna shala in Valmiki Ramayana, which is a phonetic variant of Paranh Salai in Thamizh. Paranh-Attic). For nearly 12 years they resided there. During this period Rama met various learned personalities, of whom was Ahkathiar, founder of First Thamizh Chankam (Thamizh Literary Association), was noteworthy.

Then evil appeared in the form of Soorpanaka, sister of Ravana, a cannibal.

[Anecdote of Ravana: (Excerpts from Srimad Bhaga-vatham). One evening, Kartha veerya Arjuna, Kshatriya king of Kusa dweepa (Iran), camped along with his thousand sons on the bank of a river to spend the night. When night fell, they saw Ravana and his relatives, (Mongolians of Eela Avrutham –Gobi desert) were lighting fire for human sacrifice. Immediately Arjuna's sons diverted the river water and quenched it. Fighting arose upon which Ravana and his relatives were driven away far down south through Kutch such that they could not return. Thereafter, Ravana and is his group travelled through Western Ghats (South India) far down south hiding themselves to avoid being identified, and reached a valley in Thrikoota parvatham (now called, Thirikona malai in Yazhpanam in north Sri Lanka). They named it Eelanka, i.e., limb of Eela. What is mentioned in Ramayana as Lanka is a phonetic variant of Eelanka.

They referred themselves as 'Rakshas', i.e., protectors. They captured only young men for human sacrifice, and never touched Females, children and old people.]

Soorpanaka was enamoured of the physical structure of Rama and tried to entice him, but Rama directed her to Lakshmana. Lakshmana could not tolerate her approaches, cut her nose. She felt ashamed and with vengeful mind approached Ravana and informed of what happened. As Ravana and his men knew that they could not fight with Rama at his place, and, therefore, decided to kidnap Seetha and bring her to their place, and when Rama would come to Eelanka to redeem Seetha, they would fight and kill him in their own place and avenge Soorpanaka's ignominy.

When Ravana entered Lanka with Seetha, Vibhishana, his younger brother, chided him for bringing a woman, which is against their Code and asked him to send her back to her husband. Ravana did not listen, and made her stay in Ashoka Vana (Grove for relaxation/resting). He also kept Thrijata, daughter of Vibhishana, to be on guard and to keep Company.

(According to Rakshasas, every mountain and hill range was Jata- matted hair of Lord Shiva. As such, confluence of Three hill ranges, in which Lanka was situated, was named by them as 'Thrijata'. Vibhishana'a daughter was also named as such).

While being carried away, Seetha dropped her jewels one after another to indicate the southern direction and route. While Rama and Lakshmana travelled southward direction, they met an old tribal women, referred to as Sapari (Rigteousness pervaded) who collected fruits and first bit them herself to select the sweet ones and gave them to Rama. He saw her face brightened when she bit the fruits, and ate the left-over fruits without hesitation. This place is mentioned 'Sapari Theertham', in Khammam District, Andhra Pradesh..

This trait of Rama was appreciated by the learned and praised him as the embodiment of Simplicity.

The two proceeded further and reached 'Rishya Mukha Parvatha'. (Rishya – Enlightened; Mukha- Face- here entrance; parvatha – Range of hills. This refers to hill Ranges in Gudur area in Nellore District on the East Coast., Andhra Pradesh).

There, Sugriva King of Kishkintha (Now –Solinkar, near Vellore, Tamil Nadu.), his minister, Anuman (mentioned as Hanuman) and his warriors were living in hiding.

Vaali, elder brother of Sugriva, fought with him in a wrestling bout, defeated him and drove him out. He also took over Sugriva's wife and son, Ankatha, as was the ancient custom among Tribes. In Bhagavatham they were referred to as 'Plavagendra'. Plavaga –Evolutionary stage; Indra- sensual composition of each species, Thus, the nomenclature indicates that they were ancient native/

tribe. In Ramayana they were referred to as Vaanarah- combination of two, viz., Vana – forest, and narah- human, i.e., natives living in forests. Vanaram refers to monkeys. Very many 'so called' scholars, even today refer to Sugriva, Anuman (also called 'Anchaneya') and their kinds as monkeys, that too with 'Tail'. (One can wonder whether the Ape man had a tail!).

When Sugriva saw the two warriors with bows approaching, he mistook that war may arise, and started preparations, while Anchaneya noticed that they were morose and were in search of something. After advising Sugriva to wait he went to Rama and introduced himself first and then enquired about them. Rama explained to him about their predicament and were in search of Seetha. Then Anchaneya took them and introduced to Sugriva. Here also Rama declared that, from then on, including Sugriva they were six brothers and called him to come and embrace him. While Rama sat on a small rock, Anchaneya, who was very young, sat on the ground beside him

Observing the three 'R's, i.e., Righteous thought, talk and deed in Anchaneya, which he cherished, Rama set his hand over his head and declared him as his 'Son'.

While Sugriva sent his men in different directions in search of Seetha, he specifically sent Anchaneya towards south. Rama gave him the Ring she presented at the time of their marriage and also certain incidents in their life to establish the identity that Anchaneya was Rama's messenger.

{Till 5,100 years ago Sri Lanka was a contiguous part of South India. What is now called 'Sethu sea' was a shallow landscape with gravels and pebbles spread over. On the western side was a range of hillocks and rocks. This was referred to as 'Gandha mathana Parvatham'. Gandham means Odour, in specific it refers to Sandalwood. The whole area was a virgin forest with lot of medicinal herbs grown every where. In Thamizh it was referred to as 'Kumari kantam', i.e., Virgin continent. Only Sittha physicians ventured to collect herbs, and human settlement was avoided to save pristine nature. Being a tropical forest, there was copious rain almost in all seasons. A River named

'Pahruli Aaru (river)" was flowing from this landscape, which flew on the eastern side of the hillocks and circumventing in the hills, turned westward and flowing along Tuticorin shores, reached the Indian Ocean. On the eastern side of the shallow land, sea entered, forming backwater for a short distance along what we know as Yazhpanam (Jafna). About 5,100 years ago catastrophe struck the world over. There were earthquakes, and volcanoes erupted in both Western and eastern Oceans, and enormous quantities of lava flew into the oceans, leading to excessive heat. Ice bergs melted, resulting in the rise of water level in Oceans and seas. Moreover, several landscapes, including the main Kandava Vana in the Bay of Bengal submerged by the sea. It may also be noteworthy, that, rocks rolled down in earthquake, splitting Salathy sea in West Asia into two, viz., Black sea and Caspian Sea.

In this deluge, huge and powerful waves rolled and pushed the sand from nearby sea shores an dumped in the shallow landscape, and sea water also inundated, resulting in formation of a new Sethu sea and also surrounded a big chunk of this land forming an Island, which is now called 'Sri Lanka'. In Buddha's time it was known as 'Simhala Dweepam'. Peaks of several hillocks are found as small islands, some of which are 'Rameswaram, Dhanushkoti, katchatheevu, etc.]

Anchaneya swam across the sea (backwaters) at the North east and approached Thri koota parvatha, where a Rakshasa woman was on guard. He hoodwinked her and entered the settlement, After searching he found Seetha in the grove, introduced himself, gave the wedding ring, given by Rama and also narrated the incidents, as told by Rama himself to establish his credentials. On his plea to follow him and he would take her to Rama, Seetha refused, stating that it would be an ignominy to the valour of Rama, and that she would wait for him to come and release her.

Anchaneya felt that he should not return like a coward, as Ravana did. Therefore, he broke he branches of trees creating a big scene of his presence. On Ravana's command, he was caught and brought before him. Anchaneya introduced himself as Rama's messenger. Ravana, Out of anger, sarcastically addressed him Vaanaram (animal), instead of Vanara (human). While all the eyes were set on him, Anchaneya took advantage of the weakness of their anger, mesmerized and bewildered them, grew a seemingly long tail, coiled it and sat over it at a level equal to that of Ravana. Ravana rejected the repeated request of his brother, Vibhishana, to release Seetha. Highly enraged by the action of the Vaanara, he ordered his men to wind the tail with oil-soaked cloth and light it, which was carried out. Anchaneya caught hold of the burning' cloth 'tail' and went around the Lanka settlement and burnt their residents. He then left and reached the place, where Rama and Lakhmana were waiting for him. While reaching, to avoid anxiety, the first thing he did was to shout out, 'Met Seetha, Met Seetha', and then appeared before Rama.

(Canto 9: -Ch:9 to 14 of Srimad Bhagavatham and Valmiki Ramayana)

In brief, Rama and Lakshmana, after making preparations for war, reached the sea shore, along with Sugriva, and his men. Vaanaras collected the rocks and boulders from nearby hill Ranges. They carried small rocks by hand and rolled boulders, with wooden logs, dumped them in the sea methodically, and laid a causeway. They walked over it and reached the Thrikoota Parvatham.

(Along with them, Sambavan, oldest of the ape – human species also went. Sambavan is mentioned as Jambavan in Ramayana, and also is described as a 'bear'. According to the evolution theory, Tortoise to Rhinoceros. Boar, Bear, Ape from which evolved ape- man and then human).

Ravanana came to know of Rama's Arrival and started preparations for war. Vibhishana tried to induce Ravana to release Seetha and send her to Rama. Infuriated Ravana drove Vibhishana away from the settlement, asking him to go to Rama.

As there was no place to go, Vibhishna went to Rama and sought asylum. Rama sought the opinion of those with him about granting asylum, and everyone advised in the negative. As Anchaneya was silent, Rama sought his opinion also. He too opined that, though he saw Vibhishana as a righteous person, it may not be proper to grant asylum at the time of war. **To this Rama gave his decision, that, it was only proper for a Warrior to grant asylum to anyone who sought for it, and he should face whatever consequences that may arise**. Then wholeheartedly he asked Vibhishana to come and embrace him, and declared, 'Including Vibhishana they were seven brothers'.

War was fought for nine days. Vaanaras threw stones and rocks from the hill slopes on the approaching Rakshasas, and also wrestled with many others and killed them. Everyday one Rakhasa, looking like Ravana appeared (camouflage) and he was killed. On the tenth day Ravana himself appeared and he was also killed. With this war came to an end.

[Ravana was depicted as Dasa Kanta (Ravana). In which Kanta denotes neck. Ten persons appeared nearly similar and not easy to differentiate]

As per Rama's wish, Lakshmana brought Seetha from Ashoka vana. Then Rama asked his brother to prepare a 'fire bed' and directed that Seetha walked over that bed and then come to him, Though everyone was shocked, Seetha knew Rama's intention and accordingly walked over that bed and came to Rama.

This action of Rama is a bone contention till date. Rama knew the Code of Rakshasas well and had no doubt about her chastity. But it was for Seetha to prove her innocence and chastity before the public, Moreover, after their return to Ayodhya and became the queen, the people of Ayodhya should accept her as their noble queen. From then onwards, Fire walking has become a ritual till date for truth testing and in the temples of Goddesses, especially in South India, several people of both sexes walk over fire to purify their thoughts and also establish their righteousness.

Rama, Seetha and Lakshmana were received by Bharatha and Shatrugna at Nandigrama and were led to Ayodhya.

Rama was crowned as the king of Ayodya. Noteworthy among those, who attended the coronation, was Ahkathiyar, Thamizh Laureate, who instituted the first Thamizh Chankam (Thamizh Literary Institution). This was about 7,500 years ago.

Rule of King Rama was praiseworthy and became the model code for other kings to follow.

All along, the king owned all the properties for himself, and also the Courtiers to whom the King gave away as Grants Rama's first order was giving away the ownership of lands, where educational institutes were established outside the city. Likewise, he gave away the ownership of lands, which people were using for their professional activities to themselves. **Thus, he was the first to bring in Private ownership rights over properties**.

Then litigations came up before the King. He carefully listened to both plaint and the counter, and sought the opinion of the learned and elites on each and every case. After the elites gave their opinions, he told the Court how he viewed the case and also after analyzing the elite's opinions gave his verdict. **Thus, he was the first to introduce Jurisprudence in dealing with litigations**, thereby people's say on legal proceedings were recognised.

After the proceedings of the Royal Court was over, **Rama left the crown and jewels at the Royal Court itself, as they were meant for the position as a King**, and retired to his private apartment as a common man in Dhoti and a shawl. Seetha also followed him, leaving her crown and jewels in the Royal Court itself, in simple saree and Sowmanglyam, the Marital Thread tied by Rama during their marriage.

Without depending on the administrative machinery alone, Rama moved **incognito** during nights among people of Ayodya, and got firsthand information on the social problems and their opinions/views on his Rule, and took remedial action for the welfare of the Society. **Thus, he introduced collection of intelligece on various matters concerning the Kingdom**.

During one of his movements incognito, He saw a man chiding his wife, who stayed away the previous night and returned, 'Do you think I am Rama to accept you', and sent her away. Rama realized that many people did not agree to his taking back Seetha as his wife. On return to palace he explained the incident to Lakshmana and asked him to leave Seetha – then pregnant - near the 'Pracheta Ashrama' of Valmiki. (Prachetha – birth of matured knowledge) and then inform her of what happened. Accordingly Lakshmana took Seetha near the Ashrama (hermitage), informed her of what all happened and left. On hearing this, Seetha was overtaken by grief and swooned. Later, womenfolk of the Ashrama took her to Valmiki Muni. When he could not accept Rama's action of deserting his pregnant wife, Seetha asked him not to find fault with Great soul as Rama and started narrating the biography of Rama till her being sent to the Ashrama. In due course, she left the mortal world, a few days after giving birth to twin male children. They were named. Lava and Kucha.

Valmiki Muni, admiring the greatness of Rama and Seetha, composed the biography of Rama, titled 'Ramanayam', the first Epic in Paali language, which is now known as Sanskrit. He also taught this Epic to Lava and Kucha, without informing them that they were Rama's sons. He arranged for their learning and training in Martial Arts as warriors.

The Royal horse of Rama became old, Hoofs got bent by age, and legs started trembling. Being a Royal horse it should have a Warrior's Death. The horse was taken on entourage through nearby kingdoms, led by Lakshmana and Anchaneya with a token Army. The kings of repective kingdoms paid tributes as a token as though the horse won in a war, and the entourage reached the Valmiki Ashrama. As the horse represented the king, Lava and Kucha captured the horse and challenged them to fight and release it. Lakshmana and Anchaneya realised that they were the sons of Rama. While they were trying to explain the purpose, Valmiki arrived there and appeased the twins. Then he took both of them along with others to Rama's Court. On Valmiki's direction, both of them recited 'Ramayanam' before Rama himself. While hearing the Epic, composed on Seetha's narration to Valmiki, tears rolled down, as his mind was filled with the memories of his past. After the recital was over, The twins were introduced by Valmiki to Rama as his sons.

At proper time Rama enthroned Kucha, second of his twin sons, Lava and Kucha (the one born second of the twins, is considered as elder); swam across

River Sarayu and left for Badarika Ashrama (now known as Bhadrinath) and spent rest of his life there, meditating on Sriman Narayana. As directed by hm, Lakshmana left for Kapila Theertha, at the confluence of Ganga and Sea. Anchaneya left for Kishkintha (Now known as Sholingar near Vellore in North Tamil Nadu). He sat on a hillock, facing north, meditating on Rama and left the mortal world.

From Kucha onwards, 144 names of Rama's lineage were mentioned in Bhagavatham, and that they were all praiseworthy. 141st of the lineage was Chozha (Charu in Sanskrit. He was a Great Scholar, discarded the throne and led his life as Acharya (Professor). His younger brother became the King of Ayodhya.

144th was Bruhathpalan, a Charioteer, who fought in Maha Bharatha war on the side of Dhuryodhana (Kauravas) against Pandavas, and was killed by Abhimanyu, son of Arjuna. With his martyrdom Rama's Dynasty came to an end. This was about 5,100 years ago, and by the narration in Bhagavatham, Rama's Lineage ruled for nearly 2,400 years.

It is futile to teach Great ideals of life to the common people, who cannot understand them. Rama held great virtues and righteousness as his path of life and paved the way for people to follow. All the sufferings he experienced in upholding rigteousness and virtues did not deter him at any stage. That is why the people admire him, even after 7,500 years, as a 'Guiding Star' leading them in the path of righteous life. Even today, people in many parts of North India Chant "Ram, Sathya Ram", i.e, 'Rama, Rama the righteous' (Sathyam-Righteousness).

Thus, three evolutionary steps in human progress in Life were established and termed as Mupparinama Yuhkam (Sanskrit Thretha Yugam), i.e., Tri Ordeal Evolution.

CHAPTER 22

Dual facets of Humaan concepts of Mind

Third stage of Evolution of life system and second of evolution of Human System is "Dual facets of the human concept of mind", termed, "Irunilai Parinama Yuhkam (Sanskrit- Dwapara Yugam).

Concept of mind: This is dealt with in ancient Thamizh under "Aaya Kalai Mana Iyal", the Treatise on the Concept of Mind and behavioral Attitude

In brief, the mind consists of two interlinked aspects,

1) Ahkam - inner self, and 2) Puram – External, depending on the physical senses.

Ahkam, inner self is based on three functional modes termed, 'Kun(h)am'.

The word kunham is defined as 'inducement of functions through passage of time'. [k – (consonant) first alphabet of kadappadu - passing through life; u – (undu) induce, and n(h)a – period/time factor.

Three functional modes, as the basis of mind, are as follows.

(1) **Chatthuvam**–Taking responsibility with straight forward approach. (Derivation: chatth(u) - straightforward, and va (m) – responsibility).

(2) **Vaaranam** – willingness to work for living.

(Vaa- vaazhkai - life; Anham – period/span of time; (Vaanam –life span) ra – to act, i.e., to work for living.

(3) **Thamam** - State of mind engrossed in sensuary perceptions. [Tha- first alphabet of thannilai – state of mind set; ma – first alphabet of mayankuthal – bewilderment, i.e., engrossed in sensual/emotional activities, viz., play, music, indulgent in enjoyment and physical pleasures, and also sleep.

All the three Modes are not uniformly poised at any time. Two main states of minds, each one is distinctly different from the other, are mentioned below:

a) Consciousness that he is the chief/ruler, in whom the second Mode, viz., Vaaranam takes over his mind as, 'Arrogance of power, while the third Mode, Thamam supports it, while the First one, Satthuvam takes the back seat. This person is termed as a warrior- 'Sooran' in Thamizh as well as in Sanskrit.

b) For a man of Valour, Straight forwardness as the main Mode, and, Vaaranam and Thamam are subservient to it. Such a person is denoted as Vallaan in Thamizh and Showri in Sanskrit. This person, though trained in Martial arts and well educated, does not give room for the tendency to rule over and to fight, but and remain calm, be sympathetic and be amiable to society.

Two brothers, were born to Vasudeva and Thevaki in prison, the elder one, named, Rama (known as Bala Rama) as the Warrior, i.e., Sooran, of the first State of mind-set and the younger one named, Krishna, as the Valiant, i.e., Vallavan/ Sowri, of the second State of mind-set. Krishna was also known as 'Veeran'.

Let us go through the brief history, dating back to about 5,100 years. On the Eastern Bank of Kaliya River (now known as Yamuna River), Lineages of Dhruva, praised as Kokulam (Gokulam, phonetic variant of Thamizh name), were ruling as Chieftains and Kings. In Sanskrit this Sect was referred to as 'Vaarshaneeya' Kulam.

Vasuthevan and Nanthakopan were sons of a Chieftain of Kokulam.

During the same period, King Ugrasena was ruling at Mathura, which was on the west Bank of Kalia River, now known as Yamuna.

His elder brother had seven daughters. He gave all his daughters in marriage, considering that it was a great boon to have the relationship with Kokulam.

Ugrasena had one son, elder, named 'Kamsa', and a daughter, younger, named 'Thevaki' (mentioned as Devaki in Maha Bharatham). Ugrasena also gave his daughter in marriage to Vasutheva as his <u>eighth wife</u>. Her Brother, Kamsa, took both Vasutheva and Thevaki on Chariot, driving himself, considering it an honour, and went in a procession through the streets of Mathura. While people congregated and watched, someone from the crowd shouted, "Thevaki's eighth son would kill you". (Thevaki being the eighth wife of Vasutheva). Though that person could not be located, Kamsa was shocked by those words. He drove the chariot straight to the Prison and interned them. When his parents objected, he imprisoned them also, and likewise all those, who objected.

Kamsa allowed the other wives to visit and take food to Thevaki and Vasutheva in the prison. Whenever a Child was born to Thevaki, it was taken to Kamsa, who threw the child above and held a sword below, such that the child fell on it and got killed, and thus, six children were killed by Kamsa.

When a male child was born as the seventh to Thevaki, a Child was born to Nanthakopa, younger brother of Vasutheva, at Kokulam. In order to protect the lineage of his brother, Nanthakopa brought his child and was waiting outside the prison. One of the wives of Vasutheva brought the male child secretly and gave it to Nanthakopa, and took his child into the prison. Kamsa killed this child also, mistaking it to be the child of Thevaki.

Nandakopa and his wife, Yasotha, named the child, 'Rama', and brought him up as their own son.

During the Rainy reason, in the month of Aavanhi (August-September), on the confluence of Urohini Star and eighth Waning Moon, at midnight, amidst thunder showers, eighth male child was born to Thevaki. During the same day, earlier, a female child was born to Nanthakopa. He brought that child and was waiting near the prison. One of the wives of Vasutheva brought the male child out of prison and handed over to Nanthakopa, took the female child inside the prison, and announced that a child was born to Thevaki. As usual, Kamsa killed this child also. While throwing the female child upwards, he remembered the voice and doubt arose in his mind as to how could the child be a female. From then on this doubt lingered in his mind.

Nantakopa brought the eighth son of Vasutheva to Kokulam and brought up as his own son. On the advice of Arava Muni, Naratha, The Child was named, 'Krishna'.

[Notes: Paali (Sanskrit) nomenclature, 'Krishna', is defined as the 'Core of Nature, which causes all creations'. In Thamizh the core is termed as Karu (core).

Aravam depicts the second evolutionary stage of Thamizh, when 'stroke' alphabets were introduced and documentation commenced.]

These two brothers were distinctly of two mental set up and grew up as the 'Men of Era'(messiahs) of this Evolution of Dual faceted mental set up - one as 'the one to Rule', and the other as 'the Saviour in the hour of need'. Their behavioural attitude is analysed in the following paragraphs.

Both the boys were given proper Education and training in Martial Arts. Rama, the elder, started nurturing the thought that he was to become a Ruler, and behaved in that direction. He moved with boys of his status and did not move with commeners.

Whereas, Krishna, the Younger, was friendly with all and was compassionate. His close friend was Southama, a physically handicapped, whom other boys avoided, and would do anything the latter asked for. As he was the eighth child of Thevaki, all trusted him as the one born to kill the tyrant, Kamsa. None of them did not even consider as to how this boy, who moved and played with boys, could kill Kamsa, a great warrior and a Wrestler.

This sort of belief, which is only based on sensual/emotional approach, devoid of reasoning, is termed, Devotion out of Lust (Great expectations, without putting efforts by oneself). In Thamizh, it is termed 'Kaamatthin Eadupaadu', and in Sanskrit, it is 'kaama Bhakti'.

[Note: There are four different ways of devotion, based on sentiments/ emotions, generally prevalent, as below:

1) Devotion out of enmity: (Ramayana) Ravana and his younger brother, Kumbakarna, always thinking of Rama and intent to wreck vengeance; In Mahabharatha, Shishupala (king of Chedi (later known as Kadi, Afghanistan) and his brother, Danthavakra, against Krishna,

[As they were Kshatriyas (Ruling caste), whereas, Krishna was a Shudra (Sanathani)].

2) Devotion out of fear: Kamsa against Krishna, always engrossed in mind that Krishna would kill him.

3) Devotion out of Lust: to achieve what is near impossible for oneself: Devotion of the people of Kokulam towards Krishna.

4) Devotion out of Kinship (friendship): Pandavas towards Krishna They never questioned Krishna and followed his advice/direction. To them Krishna was a 'Friend, Philosopher and Guide'.

Other than the above, there is also the "Devotion of the Enlightened".

All these five are depicted in Thamizh as follows: 1) Pahkai, (enmity) 2) Accham,(Fear) 3) Kaamam,(Lust) 4) Natpu, (Friendship) and Gnyanam (Enlightened knowledge)]

While commoners distanced from Rama, the elder, they played with Krishna and called him out of unstinted devotion as, "Kanha", and "Kanhaiya"

Kanh - Thamizh – Eye, i.e. vision; Kanhaiya –Kanh+aiya. Aiya – Term of addressing the master/leader. He was the vision and the leader of those, who were blind in the darkness of ignorance.

[Note: Nobel Laurate Albert Einstein stated in a Science Congress that, "Science without Religion (devotion) is lame, and Religion (Devotion) without Science is Blind".]

Even today people in North India, irrespective of languages they speak, worship Krishna as Kanhaiya, and Krishna Kanhaiya.

Other than the two mothers, Thevaki and Yasotha, Krishna had one more mother, Radha, his peternal aunt and sister of Nanthakopa, who nursed him with motherly affection even from his childhood. Even after marriage, she always thought of Krishna and spent most of the time with the child.

[Those, who migrated from Afganisthan and entertained Manuvada ideology, i.e., caste by birth, and were not accepted in most parts of this country, twisted and mystified Krishna's anecdotes to suit their schism. One of them is that of Radha's affection as Prema Bhakthi, i.e. Devotion out of conjugal Love. This is preposterous –how could they even think of love between aunt and nephew! Even today this preposteous schism is celebrated as Radha Krishna Kalyanam (marriage) as a Relegious festival in the North.].

Kamsa came to know that Thevaki's eighth son, Krishna, was brought up by Nanthakopa at Kokulam. The so-called prophesy haunted him, and he clandestinely devised several means to kill that child. They were all thwarted by the watchful vigil of Kokulam people. When he was five year old, to keep away from the machinations of Kamsa, Nanthakopa led all the people far away to 'Virunthu Vanam' (Brinda vanam) and temporarily stayed till Rama and Krishna were old enough to take care of themselves.

(Virunthu –Thamizh word – Guest as well as feast. During festivals people congrated here and had fun and feast. Settlements were avoided here, as this was the place were Thiruvan (Dhruva did penance fixing his mind in Lord Narayana, and as such, considered 'Serene'. This place is referred to in Thamizh literatures as 'Aayar Paadi'. Aaya Kalai means Treatises based on higher studies. Hence, Aayar referred to those, who had gained higher knowledge. Paadi means camp. As such, this place was referred to as the "Camp/Congregation of the people seeking higher knowledge".

In Aayar paadi, the boys were trained initially in Physical Training in Acrobatics (Thamizh-Udarpayirchi; Sanskrit-Vyayaamam), then stick fencing, and wrestling to those physically fit, followed by Archery and sword fighting.

(Acrobatics, stick fencing and Wrestling were National Games throughout this Country. Very few are taught about 15 Nadis- nerve systems, i.e., 5 sets each of 1) Monitoring senses-Than maathiram, 2) Sciatic-gnyana Manthiram, and 3) Motor Nerves- Kata Manthiram, and various intricate postions in the physique. This enabled a wrestler to protect himself, and at the same attack the other to disable this system. This part is mentioned as Nadik kalai,(today referred to as Acupuncture) which was also practiced by physicians.)

Both Rama and Krishna became experts in these martial arts. As Rama became expert in wrestling, he was then called 'Bala Rama' (Balam-Sanskrit; Strength. Thamizh - Sooran) Thus, in History there were three men in named 'Rama', viz., Parasu Rama, Ragu Rama, and Bala Rama.

Krishna, because of his composure, not exhibiting his strength and amiable to all sections of people, was praised as 'Vallaan' ('val', and 'laan'- two syllables), and also 'Veeran'-Man of valour (Sanskit – Showri).

Kamsa's mind was haunted by the thought of Krishna, was always counting the age of Krishna. When the latter attained 14 years of Age, he sent his minister, Akroora to Aayar padi (Brindavan), to invite and also bring Bala Rama and Krishna to take part in a festival. Though Nanthakopa and others were hesitant, they respected the minister and sent them both to Mathura.

Both of them went round Mathura on sight seeing. Krishna noticed an Armory, where a Bow made of Stone was kept at the entrance as an indication. Krishna lifted this bow, and when he tried to bend it to hook up the bow string, it broke off. This incident was conveyed to Kamsa. He took this as a Challenge and called Krishna for Wrestling fight, Though Balarama, being elder, offered himself for a fight, Kamsa declared that it was between himself and Krishna as he committed the crime of entering the Armory, and, by breaking the bow, he had challenged self (Kamsa). Moving fast during the fight, Krishna pressed Kamsa's toe, arresting his movement, and holding Kamsa's back on his knee, broke his Spinal chord and thus Kamsa was killed. Then He went to the prison, released Ugrasena and the queen, and also his own parents, Vasutheva and Thevaki. Ugrasena was re-enthroned as the rightful King of Mathura.

Krishna did not claim the throne as a right, since he defeated the King by killing him in fight, but was contented that he fulfilled the aspirations of the people.

He never returned to Kokulam thereafter.

Afterwards, both Bala Rama and Krishna were sent to 'Chandeepani' Ashrama (Seat of higher knowledge) and continued their education.

Even here, while Bala Rama moved with princes, as it was his attitude, Krishna made intimate friendship with Suthaama, who was from a family of Learned, and both were discussing on various branches of knowledge.

[Note: In this Ashrama, he gained expertise in 'Mupporul', also known as Pallavam, (Trifold great truth/theory on the Core of Nature, and methodical steps by Self Priming, etc.

This was translated into Paali/Sanskrit and termed Thathva Thrayam, known as 'Sankyam'. The Bhagavath Geetha consisting of Krishna's Revelations to Arjuna in Kurukshetra on the eve of Maha Bharatha War, is based mainly on this 'Pallavam/ Sankyam'. This is relevant even today, as the Code of Sanaathanam].

After completing their studies, Bala Rama and Krishna got married.

Krishna went along with his wife, Sathya Bhama, to Kutcham (Crude landscape, now known as Kutch, South Eastern part of Gujarat) to build a City for his father, Vasutheva, to Rule. While clearing the Kaaleeya Vana ('the forest of ancient times'), he found lot of deserted women afflicted by leprosy, suffering with their children without proper food and clothing. **He took upon himself as his duty**, to alleviate those women. While he prepared medicines, his wife Sathya Bhama, nursed them with motherly care, bathed and dressed them with clean clothes and applied medicines prepared by Krishna, and cured them. He built a City, named it, 'Dwaraka' (Gate/entrance, also Vaikuntam), in which he provided residences for these women and also made arrangements for their living.

In the Early morning, before Sunrise, of Samvacchara month of Ayippasi, i.e., October 16/17 – November 14/15, on the 14th Vaning moon day, these women lit lamps in their new houses and occupied them. For them Krishna was the beacon light.

<u>**From then on, till date, this day, every year, the 14th Vaning moon day of Ayippasi month is celebrated as 'Theepa Olhi' festival.**</u> (Deepavali is the phonetic variant of Theepa Olhi; Thee –fire, and theepa is the short form of 'thee pandam, i.e., fire torch. Olhi – light.)

[Notes: In Mahabharatha, Krishna Dwaipayana (known as Veda Vyasa). mentioned about women, afflicted by Leprosy, with a poetic touch, thus: '16,100 women were imprisoned by Narakaasura, born of 'Bhoomadevi' Goddess of the Earth. This goddess was born as Sathya Bama, who killed him, while Krishna drove the Chariot for her.'. Krishna Dwaipayana, a Yeti, i.e. sub-human bear living in Imaya (mentioned as Himalayas) Ranges, did not follow human epithets and sentiments, and found everything as natural. Innate meaning of 'Narakaasura' is as follows: Narakam is psychological term referring to living physique. Na-subservience; ra-performance/activities; ka- the physique passing through life span; m-case ending. As such it depicts, 'the physique, which cannot decide on its own but subservient in its activities'.

Asuran: Asu- Oxygen; Irukanh Asu- bivalent oxygen, and mukkan Asu-Trivalent oxygen, i.e., Ozone. Asura depicts the activity of 'Asu', viz., it is so aggressive that it can oxidize even the Radio active particles and convert them into residuary particles. Any aggressive action with firm grip is denoted as 'Asuram'.

Leprosy is so much aggressive over the human physique, that, it was denoted as 'Narakaasura'.

The story of Narakasura, born to the Goddess of Earth, is wild mystic imagination to suit one's own schism, which is devoid of truth.

City of Dwaraka built by Lord Krishna for his father, Vasudeva, to rule. This city sank into the Sea during the Catatrophe which rocked the world about 5,100 years ago.

Sea Shore, Beyt Dwaraka. From this shore tourists/pilgrims go by boats, during 'Low Tides', to have a view of Sunken Dwaraka City.

The Epic titled, 'Maha Bharatham', pertained to the part of historical events in India about 5,100 years ago, and it had no relevance to the Code of life or traditions of the people of Bharatham-India. Kuru vamsa rulers were Yakshas, mainly migrants from Afghanisthan and Parsia(Iran) claiming themselves to be Vaishnavas. They followed the Manuvada varnasrama Dharma, i.e., Caste by birth. They consisted of three main castes, viz., Brahmana, Kshatriya and Vaisya. Termed "Saavarni". While Brahmana is supreme, Kshatriya can punish others, and no one can punish them. Only a kshatriya can punish the other by waging war and defeating/killing him. This led to their licentious life, devoid of moral bnding. Brahmanas were offered largessees to keep them in good humour and to support them. They ruled in few pockets in North India while the South was free of them.]

Paanchaalam was a country, which is now called Punjab. While West Punjab is in Pakisthan, the East of it is Punjab state, India. A portion of this Punjab also was carved out, and Hayana State was formed in recent times.

Panchalam was ruled by Kokulam sect (Varshaneeya Kulam). Drupada (i.e., Dru –Druva, and pada-step, i.e., the lineage of Druva) was the king of Paanchaalam during the period of Maha Bharatham. He had a son, Drushtadhyumna, and a daughter, Krishna. As the people recognized only one by this name, i.e., the son of Vasutheva, she was called. 'Draupathi', the daughter of Drupada, and also 'Paanchaali', the Princess of Paanchaalam.

Draupathi had proper eduction and training. When she attained proper age, Drupada arranged for her 'Swayamvaram', to get a suitable match for his daughter.

(Swayamvaram was in vogue in Royal families of this country in which a prince should establish his valour and competence to be accepted by the princess for marriage).

In the middle of a pond, prepared for the purpose, a post was erected over which a wheel was revolving. One image of a fish was fixed to this wheel as a target. The suitor should look into the water of the pond, observe the image of the rotating fish in it, aim the target, shoot an arrow and hit it.

Bala Rama and Krishna, Draupathi's cousins, sat alongside the King Drupada to watch the proceedings.

Dhuryodhana, prince of Hasthinapuram, attended it with his close friend, Karna.

(Brief history: Dhrutharastra, the eldest son of Sathyavathy, wife of Santhanu, of Kuru Dynasty, took over as King of Hasthinpuram. As he was born blind, His younger brother, Pandu, ruled on his behalf. He was afflicted by Leukoderma at birth itself and his name itself indicated it.

Bhishma, their paternal uncle, who was celibate, won Gandhari, the princess of Gandhara kingdom (Kandahar in Afghanisthan). in swayamvara and got her married to Dhrutharashtra, the blind King. After marriage, Gandhari did not want to see anything that her husband could not, and, therefore, tied her eyes with a cloth and remained so throughout. Her elder brother, Sakhuni, could not tolerate this, and took Bhishma as his arch enemy. Taking a owe to destroy the Kuru dynasty, which Bhishma wanted to protect, he stayed with his sister in Hasthinaouram,

Dhrutharashta begot 100 children, of whom, Dhryodhana, the eldest, Duhsasana, and a girl were born to the queen Gandhari, and the remaining 97 were born through other women in his harem. Since they were born in Kuru Vamsa, they were termed 'Kauravas'.

Since Dhrutharastra was born blind, his younger brother, Pandu ruled on his behalf. Pandu had two wifes, Kunthi and Madri. Since he became potentially invalid, his wife Kunthi begot three sons, Udhishtra, Arjuna and Bheema. Through some other men. On Pandu's request, Kunthi arranged a male partner to Madri also, and she gave birth to two sons, Nahula and Sahadeva. Since the two women were the wifes of Pandu, the five sons were recognized as his sons, and were called, 'Pandavas'.

Kunthi begot a male child before marriage. As, such a birth is not socially acceptable and considered illegitimate, she tore a portion of her upper garment, covered the child and kept it in a basket and floated it in the river. While doing so, she kept a Chest Armour and Ear Rings worn by warriors, in the basket, as an identification that the child was born to a warrior. Sanjaya, the Chariot driver of Dhrutharashta, who went to the river to bathe, found the basket with the child, and took it home. He named the Child as 'Karna', and got him trained in martial arts, mainly in archery.

Royal princes grew up. Annual Sports Meet in Martial Arts was held, in which Kauravas and Pandavas took part. Karna tried to take part in it. Arjuna, second of the Pandavas, objected to his participation, stating that Karna was not a Kshatriya. Dhuryodhana, who was jealous of Pandavas, took this opportunity and declared Karna 'a Kshatriya', and took him oover to his side. Once declared Kshatriya, Karna was always waging wars against various kingdoms, as it was the Kshatriya Dharma, shedding blood everywhere and looted. He then gave major portions of the looted property as Daana (benevolence) to Brahmanas. Pleased with this generosity, they praised him as 'Daana, veera, soora Karna', ignoring the fact that it was the looted property which they had received as Daana. According to them, it was Kshatriya Dharma to wage war. Unfortunately this kind of notion continues to persist even today.. He was loyal to Dhuryodhana, since it was he, who gave him the status of a Kshatriya. He also nurtured enmity towards Pandavas, especially Arjuna.

In due course, Pandu died, and the question arose as to who should rule. While one section was of the view that, Yudhishtra, son of Pandu, being elder, could be declared as the Prince, Sakuni declared that since Dhrithaashtra (blind) was the king and his eldest son, Dhuryodhana was of the age (above 18 years), he should be declared the prince and he could rule on behalf of his blind father. His writ prevailed and Dhuryodhana became the Prince. Pandavas left the palace and moved to a village. Sakhuni devised a plan to annihilate Pandavas, since they would create problems any day for Dhuryodhana's Rule. He got a 'wax' building constructed. He then sent for Pandavas to take part in a festival, and arranged for their stay in the wax building. Vidhura, a step brother of Dhrutharashtra, was righteous and secretly dug a tunnel and asked Pandavas to escape through that, at night after explaining the machination of Sakuni. He also arranged for a servant maid to stay in that wax building along with her five sons. Without knowing these developments, Sakuni set the building on fire. While Pandavas and Kunthi escaped through the tunnel, the servant maid and her five sons were charred to death. Next day sakuni saw the dead bodies, mistook them to be Pandavas, and was greatly relieved that the Pandavas were annihilated. Afterwards, pandavas moved about disguising themselves as Brahmanas. Now we can move on to the scenario of Draupathi's Swayamvara.]

Pandavas too came there under the guise as Brahmanas.

Several princes tried their luck to shoot the target in fish-form and failed. Karna got up to try, But Draupati objected to his taking part in it, stating that he was the son of a charioteer. Karna felt ashamed and retreated. He then decided to avenge her at an opportune time.

Arjuna, second of the Pandavas, tried and succeeded in shooting down the fish form. This was a great feat, and by this deed Arjuna and other Pandavas were exposed. Prior enmity of Kauravas raised its ugly head, and the ignominy of Karna was added to it.

Bala Rama made friendship with Dhuryodhana as he was a prince. Later on he gave training to the latter in various technics in wrestling and made him a master in that martial art. But he did not take note of the happenings at swayamvara.

But Krishna, the younger, keenly watched the developments, viz., Karna being humiliated and Draupathi's acceptance of Arjuna, the Pandava. He foresaw the danger lurking to Draupathi, and decided to protect her. He voluntarily introduced himself to Pandavas and went along with Draupathi and Pandavas to their residence.

On reaching the residence, Arjuna called out to his mother telling that he has brought 'Phalam'. The word, Phalam denotes fruit as well as the 'fruition of effort'. While coming out, she asked them to share it equally. After she saw Draupathi, she realized her mistake and asked them to ignore what she said. As what was told remained in mind, Pandavas took her as their equal and she would also share what all they got/achieved. Krishna noticed this also as one more predicament. On his advice, Pandavas moved out, leaving Draupathi with their mother, Kunthi, travelled to various places to gain friends and support.

Since Draupathi was treated equal, Krishna helped Arjuna to marry his sister, Subhadhra. On his direction Arjuna took her to Draupathi for acceptance. Though shocked initially that Arjuna deserted her, she realized the situation and accepted their marriage, thereby Subhadhra's son, Abhimanyu, got the legal status to claim the throne later.

Each of the other Pandavas married a woman and arranged to bring up one of the sons, born to them as the son of Draupathi (Draupathi Puthra).

Arjuna too married the princess Aravalli (Southwest of Mathura in Rajasthan; People's spoken language was Ancient Thamizh, known as Aravam), and princess of Manipur (North East India). The sons of these two were brought up as sons of Draupathi. In total, there were six sons brought up as the Sons of Draupathi.

(This part of history is mentined in Srimad Bhagavatham, and not found in 'Mahabharatham'. Draupathi remained spinster throughout. While this is the fact, those, who praise Karna has been propagating till date that she was the wife for all the five Pandavas. It is certainly preposterous, though, the gullible people believe this evil infested story.)

In the meanwhile, Vidhura, step brother of the king, appealed to the king Dhrutharashtra to give away a portion of the Kingdom for Pandavas to Rule, as their father, Pandu, was a Ruler. Prince Dhuryodhana rejected it and stated that they could go to Kandava vana and rule there.

(Gauntuwana, as mentioned in present history is a phonetic variant of the Thamizh nomenclature, Kandava vana. Details of this island are furnished earlier.)

Krishna too felt that Pandavas too should have a place to Rule, and arranged for building "Indraprastha" in Kandava vana by "Paramacharya Mayan". (Acharya- professor; Paramacharya-Eminent professor). The wonders of the palace were mentioned in Mahabharatham itself, viz., highly polished granite stone floors, glass panes as screens, mentioned as spaticum, etc. (spaticum- crystal, i.e., glass. Thamiz- Aati).

Krishna also got a Disc weapon, made by the Paramacharya Mayan, – mentioned as Chakra ayudham. This was the one mentioned as 'Chakrayudham' in Maha Bharatham, and mystified as Vishnu Chakram.

In brief, Kauravas and other kings of the North attended the'Yaga' ceremony, organized by the Pandavas to take over rule in Indraprastha. Jealousy played, and pandavas were invited to Hasthinapura, where Yudhishtra, fond of gambling, started playing Dice game with Sakuni, in which he lost everything. Finally, though he had no right, pledged Draupathi also and lost. None of those in the assembly noticed the presence of Krishna, who was by her side. On orders of Dhuryodhana, his younger brother Dhuhsasana dragged her by her lock of hair and brought her before the congregation. Dhuryodhana asked her to sit on his lap, and Karna, the loyal, commented that there was nothing wrong being the wife of five, to sit on his friend's lap. This did not happen. Then Dhuhsasana started to pull out her saree on the orders of his elder brother, but Krishna mesmerized the congregation. imagining that he was pulling out her saree, Duhsasana tried his best, but failed.

Then Draupathi, having been humiliated in public, took the vow to tie her lock of hair with the blood from the lap of Dhuryodhana, on which he asked her to sit. Bheema took the vow that he would avenge by breaking the thigh of Dhryodhana.

Then Dhuryodhana declared that the Pandavas should live in forest for 12 years and one more year to live incognito, and then claim Indraprastha. Accordingly pandavas moved about in forests. Attempts were made by Kauravas and their kith and kin to locate and annihilate them, and also on the honour of Draupathi but were foiled by the vigilant Pandavas. During 13th year they went to the palace of Virata king and stayed incognito. Draupathi was a companion to the queen. Udhishtra befriended and kept company in playing Dice and Chaturanga (chess), a favourite game of the Royal. Arjuna disguised himself as a woman, by name, Bruhan-nala and taught Dancing to the Prince Uttara. Bhima took over as a cook, and Nakula and sahadeva worked as Horse grooms in the Royal Stable.

Later, Abhimanyu, son of Arjuna and Subhadra, married Utthira.

During the last days of their incognito life, Keechaka, brother of the queen of Virata, arrived. Upon seeing Draupathi, he got enamoured of her, and tried to entice her. She could not stand this and complained to Bheema. As per his advice she asked Keechaka to meet her at night at the palace garden. It happened to be the last day of their incognito period. Accordingly, Keechaka arrived at the Garden and met her. When he tried to make approaches, Bheema pounced on him and fist fight ensued. Though Keechaka was a Wrestler, he was no match to Bheema and got killed by the latter in the fight. By this, Bheema and pandavas were exposed. Next day, i.e., after completion of thirteen years, it was known that they were Pandavas living in the Virata palace. This was intimated to Dhuryodhana, who, depending on Lunar Calender, refused to accept it, stating that they were exposed a few hours before completing the period. He declared that they could redeem their land by waging a war.

Krishna went as emissary of Pandavas to King Dhrutharashtra and appealed to avoid war and requested to give them, five towns, five villages, or atleast five pieces of land for them to build houses and live. But the Prince Dhuryodhana rejected them all decared that war was the only solution.

Preparations started on both sides. Arjuna met Krishna and sought his company and support, which was readily agreed by the latter. Dhuryodhana met him later, to whom Krishna gave away his Army. Balarama also gave his Army to Dhuryodhana, but personally stayed away from the war between the cousins.

Both sides met at Kurukshetra (Battlefield of Kuru Clan). On the side of Kauravas, Bheeshma, the Celebate and the eldest of Kauravas and Pandavas, Kripa, Guru, who taught Manudharma based Varnasrama and Kshatriya Dharma to both the sides, Dhrona, who trained both sides in martial art, Karna, close associate, Dhuryodana and his brothers, and Kings, who supported Kauravas, formed the front line. Archers and warriors fell in line behind them.

On the opposite front, Pandavas and kings, who supported them, formed the front line, and their warriors formed the rear.

Lord Krishna was the chariot Driver for Arjuna, the charioteer, (fighter from Chariot, mentioned as Maharathi). He drove the chariot to the war field and postioned it in front of Bheeshma. While travelling to the battle fied, Arjuna's mind dwelled in the thought of strategies to be adopted against the highly skilled Bheshma, Dhrona, Kauravas and various kings on their side and win. But when he saw them all in front, especially, his Grand father, Bheeshma, after thirteen long years of separation, he forgot that as a warrior, he should fight when challenged. Fickle minded he was, that his mind was overcome by emotions and was upset that he was to fight against them. He laid down his bow (Kanteepa), kneeled down with his head resting on his palm, and started lamenting, that had to commit great sins in killing Bheesham, his grand father,

Guru, Acharya, brothers, and friends and others, leading to destruction of (Manuvaada) Varnashrama, and finally that it would be better to go as sanyasi (saint) than to rule after committing all the sins.

Krishna watched him and heard his lamentation, which was not appropriate for a warrior, and that it was his duty to fight in the battlefield, when challenged. **He felt it was his duty to remove these irrelevant thoughts of sensual relationships and make him realize his responsibility and duty to fight in the battlefield. He started on his own to advise and make him realize to perform his duty to fight, when challenged, and not to withdraw as a coward. His address to Arjuna at the Battle field is revered as the immortal "Psalm of the Divine", "The Bhagavat Geetha".** (The full title of it is, "Bhagavath Geetha-su-Upanishath").

("The Bhagavath Geetha" with English translation is published by 'Geetha prachar Trust, Gorakhpur, Uttar Pradesh, India)

Though the Psalm was to a bewildered warrior to overcome the sensual perceptions, it is a wonderful preaching to anyone of bewildered mind, dwelling in darkness of sensual perceptions, and awakens him/her to realize himself and perform one's duty. Religious zealots declare that he is the incarnation of Lord Vishnu. **But he identifies himself in Geetha (Chapter –"Kshetram Kshetra Yogam"), that He is 'Kshetra Gnya' in 'Kshtram'.**

Kshetram is a phonetic variant of Thamizh word, 'Che(y)tthiram. Che(y)-Che-mature+Ay-cherish, i.e., matured and cherished; th- Base of knowledge; thiram – capability (of mind), - Capability of matured and cherished knowledge. Gnya is a combination of two alphabets, Gn –(consonant- Enjoin, and Ya - (Iyam as a word) - function. Thus Gnya- enjoin and function Thus by identifying himself as 'Kshetthra Gnya', **Krishna revealed that he was a Tool, functioning by enjoining the matured and cherished knowledge within.**

'Knowledge is pristine and divine', and as such the learned cherish the psalm as 'the Psalm of the Divine', and glorify Lord Krishna as 'Geethaacharya' (Acharya – Enlightened professor).

The war went on for fourteen days and the Kauravas were annihilated. Pandavas took over as Rulers of Hasthinapura. Draupathi was given equal status in administration.

Note: It is worth mentioning that Bruhathpala, King of Ayodhya and 144th in the lineage of Rama (Dasaratha's son), fought in Kurukshetra war, on the side of Kauravas and was killed by Abhimanyu. With his death, the direct rule of Rama's lineage at Ayodhya for about 2,400 years was over.

After his mission to protect Draupathi was over, Lord Krishna returned to Dwaraka, and never visited Hasthinapura again. He was above 65 years of age at that time.

[Brief History: Abhimanyu was killed during the war. His wife, Utthira, who was pregnant at the time of the war, gave birth to a son, named Parikshith. When he attained 18 years of age, Parikshith was enthroned as King of Hasthinapura. Thereafter, Pandavas and Draupathi left for Badarikaashrama (now called Badrinath, northern-most point of Imayakootam (Himalayas) to spend the remaining part of their life, surrendering their mind and soul at the lotus feet of Shriman Narayana to attain liberation.

After about 20 years, three Yetis, Krishna Dwaipayana (Known as Vedavyasa), Maithreya, and Sukha, who wrote Maha Bharatham as dictated by Dwaipayana, left Naimisa Aranya (abode of Yetis, on the Bank of Komathi river), and reached Badarikaasrama, to spend the remaining part of their life, surrendering their mnd and soul at the feet of Sriman Narayana and attain salvation.

Badarikaasrama was also known as **Panchavati**, i.e., five Steps of his own as Vasudeva (one yielded vasus-Basic particles), himself as Athyaman (Sanskrit-Pradhyumna), Kallhazhakar in Kallhazhaku (Madhava in Madhuvana), Kovintha as adiappan (Govinda as Adipurusha), and Thirumaal as appan (Vishnu as Purusha) from which evolution of Atom, etc., commenced in the Universe.

The place was also known as **Naaratha Chae(y)tthiram.** (Na- nothingness, i.e., massless; +nara- Human, the highest of the creation in nature, and tha- theism, i.e., knowledge; Cheytthiram- capability of matured and cherished knowledge. Thus the word implies, 'Capability of knowledge of creation from massless state to human, the nature's sureme creation. The enlightened professor at this seat was known as **Naaratha Muni.** Sanathana (Sanskrit-Shudra) Acharyas (Enlightened professors) from the South decorated this Seat. Lot of rare and valuable documents of Paali language, later declared as Sanskrit, viz., Upanishads, Sesha samhita, Gignyaasa, etc., were kept and protected here.]

After reaching Badarikaasrama, Krishna Dwaipaayana (Vyasa) was sitting morose. Naratha Muni approached him and addressed, "Should you not be proud that you have rendered the great histrical episode on Kuru vamsa (clan)! May be you are depressed, because you have woven the unethical and immoral life of Kuru clan with Vedic scripts, and the posterity may take it granted that it is the way of life. Now that you are all here, you may compile all the existing documents of treatises, history, etc., and document them for posterity. Lord Krishna is a great Soul. You have corrupted his greatness by including it with that of licentious life of the Kuru Clan. While compiling, make out a seperate canto depicting Krishna's biographical sketch".

Vyasa and the other two listened to his advice attentively. Vyasa asked as to what made him come to Badarikaasrama. To this Naratha replied that when he was a child, his father died, and his mother worked as servant maid in an Achrya's residence. Learned personalities used to visit and discuss on innate truths of different subjects. He used to sit with them and listened to their discussions attentively. One day, while milking a cow, his mother was bitten by a snake and died. Having been orphaned, he left that place and after wandering through various places, finally reached Badarikaasrama.

After the above conversation, Vyasa, Maithreya, and Sukha started compiling all that was documented, as Puranas (ancient ones), Upanishads

(Discussions consisting of innate truths rendered by enlightened professors), history, creation and evolution of nature, Geographical depicton, with the clans living in those places, Gods worshipped by them, etc., codified them into Cantos (Kaantams), each consisting of narrations into Chapters. Sukha jotted them all.

Vyasa rendered the first two Cantos under the pen name, 'Baadarayana', i.e., rendered during the period of his stay in Badarikaasrama. Then he left the mortal World.

Maithreya's narrations consisting of history, crearion and evolution of Nature, stellar compex, etc., formed the next three cantos. After this, Maithreya too left the mortal World.

Thereafter, Sukha wrote the remaining 6th to 18th Canto. This Documentation (Thamizh–Kaappiyam; Sanskrit–Grantha) was titled, **"Shrimad Bhagavatham"**.

By then the whole world was struck by Catastrophe. Volcanoes erupted, leading to melting of ice bergs and increase of sea levels. Earthquakes and tremors too rocked the world,. Several landscapes, and low lying areas submerged, leading to formation of islands and land raised in few places. Rocks fell and the Salathi sea (middle east) was split into two as Black sea and Caspian sea. This went on for a few years, changing the landscapes

During this period Dwaraka too started submerging. The relatives and family members of Lord Krishna died, and he was left alone. He then left Dwaraka and travelled in a chariot driven by his boyhood friend, Uddhava, and reached the Bank of 'Saraswathi' River. He climbed down from the chariot, lied down on the bank of the river, resting his head on the root of a Baniyan tree, facing north, and told Uddhava that he could leave. But the latter stayed there with Lord Krishna. He was about 101 years old by then, and waited to leave the mortal world.

In the meanwhile, Maithreya, while putting down narrations in Shrimad Bhagavatham, commenced with the history of ancient times, i.e., 10,000 years ago. In this canto he covered the discourse of Chitthar Kapilar (mentioned as Siddha Kapila in Sanskrit) to his mother, known as 'Sankya Upanishatham', when she requested him to reveal the true path of life.

Initially, he imparted in detail the truth that Shriman Narayana as the absolute one, and the necessity to surrender at his lotus feet as it was the only way to attain liberation. To this she replied that she could not understand it as she was a housewife, and requested him to impart the knowledge such that she could understand. Then, he started detailing as below (Only a brief, and not verbatim depiction):

"During the first month fetus is formed, but it does not wake up.

During second month Vaayuu (gases) enjoins it; but it does not wake up.

During third month Varuna enjoins it, but it does not wake up,

During fourth month Ahani (Sanskrit Agni; Energy) enjoins it, but does not wake up.

During fifth month Indhra enjoins it, but does not wake up.

During sixth month 'Ahankaaram' (identifying self) enjoins it, and then it wakes up and the head of the fetus turns right and downward.(and continued detailing 7th and 8th and so on) During the nineth month, the fetus suffers by the pressure of mother's stomach while breathing and the stench from its own excreta and urine. If it could only feel and speak, it would pray to the Almighty, "Oh, Lord, should I be born with all this suffering!"

During tenth month the child is born with great pain and suffering while its head squeezed through the narrow bone. But, soon after the birth, the child forgets all the pain. When grown up, the man indulges in various activities, as though he is permanent. When he is old and before dying, the mind loosing control over the body and senses begins to remember what all he had done, and suffers profusely.

The pain before birth cannot be avoided. But he can avoid the pain at the time of death, if only he lives righteously and with restraint."

Maithreya could not understand the innate truths of Varuna, Agni, Indhra, etc.. To learn about them, he set out from Badarikaasrama in search of Lord Krishna, as he was the only Acharya to impart the Innate truths on the subject. He met the Lord and beseeched to teach the innate truths of Creation (Thamizh-Padaippin nunmai; Sanskrit- Srshti Sookshmam).

[Note: Thevam– Thaa (theism)-all pervading knowledge, to know matters; e-enablement, va(vaham)- responsibility, and m-case ending. The word thus denotes the one that is responsibe to know/learn all around. They are perennial waves, e.g., light waves- chudar aazhi.]

The Lord Krishna commenced thus: "Impart this to Vidhura also."

"Thevams are minute (microcosmic). If they acted individually, and when they face one other on their path, they may destroy each other. Therfore they are destined to be in clusters (Thamizh-Kathir; Sanskrit-Ganhaah, i.e., Rays.).

"Indhra can be seen as lightning. He passes upto ear as Indhra and from the ear he reaches the brain as 'Chandra' (Sound reverberation).

(Indhra - Electric Charge. Chanda - Audition, and Chandra- sound reverberation taking place in ear lobe. Some quarters twisted the meaning of this word, and misinterpreted that Chandra denoted Moon. This falsehood is established and is prevelant even today).

"Indhra is Loka Pala.
(Human is referred to as Loka, i.e., the world. This is psychological depiction. Pala(Thamizh) - to nurture and support. As already seen above, here Indra refers to the Static Elecricity generated in glands, etc. The nerves are triggered by this electricity, and is carried as reverberations to the brain.).

"Varuna Devatha in Runa Karma.

(Varunan-Ionisation in Glands and in process of digestion, during which Static eletricity is also generated).

"Charma Devatha from Shareeram.

(Odour spread from the skin)

"Atchini devatha in Eye.

(Atchini- Spectrum. In Sanskrit - Akshini, Phonetic variant of Thamizh word).

"Aswini Deva" in nostrils.

(Fragrance; smelling sense in general).

"Agni" in Hrudayam.

(Phonetic variat of Thamizh – Ahani. –Dissipation of Energy. Its charasterics are, Patruthal-To catch, Patarthal-to spread; Seer Aathal- To neutralize. Hrudayam – Heart.

Some important Ahanis are: - Sankara Ahani-Gamma Ray; Savitha Ahani-Karia sivantha alai-Infra Rad Ray; Uruthira Ahani – Karia Sivantha-Neela Kathirveechu –Ultra violet Ray, Aataka Ahani –Lava (Volcano); Amila Ahani –Acid; Asava Ahani – alkalines and alcohols; Kirutthika Ahani – oxidation; Thaava Ahani- forest fire..

yaahka Ahani – fire in kilns, hearths, etc. Manai Ahani- Neruppu, domestically used, namely for cooking, lighting, etc. (Matha Ahani –also mentioned as Kirthikai- behavioural attitudes, viz., egoistic approach based on schisms, Lust, anger, jealousy, enmity, etc.)

"There are three veekshas – Brahma veeksha, Kaaksha, and Aan Veeksha.

(Veeksha is a phonetic variant of Thamizh word Veechu, meaning, 'spread out'. Brahma Veeksha – Thamizh-Muhar veechu, smelling sense for identification. Sanskrit word Brahmam denotes 'Clearly knowing; here identification.' Kaaksha, a phonetic variant of Thamizh – Kaatchi. Ka-refers to physic that performs (katam), Aatchi- atchini(spectrum), that enables seeing vividly of three dimentions, viz., length, width and depth; Aanveeksha – Phonetc variant of Thamizh –Aan veechu. A+An=Aan. A-akaram the prime Core of Nature; mentioned in other languages as allaahu, al-alluiah, etc.; An-Core word-Prime concept of control. Thus 'Aan Veechu' depicts 'the one that is spread out by the Core of Nature under its own prime control'. Thevams, i.e., Natural Waves created by Nature, spread out everywere and induces various activities; of them is the most important 'Olhi kathir'-the light rays'. Less said about it, the better. The English Language carries the apt term, "Vision of Knowledge".

After receiving clarifications, Maithreya returned to Badarikaasram to coninue his task of compilation of Bhagavatham.

After this discourse, Lord Krishna, having spent a purposeful life, repaid his indebtedness to the Almighty Nature, Thevams, and his ancestors, great seers, who imparted great and valuable knowledge for the humanity, left the Mortal World and attained eternity. **In commemoration of him, Saraswati River was glorified as 'Krishna Theertham', and later, as 'Krisna River'.**

(Theertham-Clear off debts-The place, were the enlightened people deliver knowledge on subjects of importance, and by this clear their indebtness as detailed above. and leave the mortal world)

Lord Krishna was also praised as Yaamuna and Yaamuni.

Ya-(Iyam as a word)- function; Muna/Muni- The one, who finds a work to be performed, takes responsibility, concentrates and puts all his efforts and performs, is called "Muni". The Lord himself depicts it in Bhagavath Geetha, while explaining the importance of performing Duty. His life, notwithstanding teaching, was that of a Muni. As such he was praised 'Yaamuna'. He was born in Mathura prison, on the western bank of Kaaliya River, and he was protected and brought up at Kokulam, on the Easten Bank of the river. This river was also named and called, **Yamuna River**, after him.

Brief history.- After a few years of rule of Parikshith, the effects of the Catastrophe, that struck the World, was also felt as Earth tremors at Hasthinapura. The King, courtiers and the people congregated at the open space on the Bank of the nearby River. In the meanwhile, after completing Shrimad Bhagavatham, Suka left Badarikaasrama and reached Naimisa Aaranya. Yeti Sootha, next to Suka in the Vyasa lineage, joined him and both went to Hasthinapura. There Sootha introduced Suka to King Parikshit. Thereupon, Suka started narrating all the 18 Cantos of Shrimad Bhagavatham without break for several days. Sootha listened to the narrations attentively and once the narrations were over, he left the place for Naimisa Aaaranya. Later, Earth Tremor struck the Area in which Hasthinapura, the King, his courtiers, people and also Suka perished.

(It was mentioned that a small serpant attacked, wherein the serpant referred to is a small branch of seismic line passing through Kaarakoram.).

With this the evolution of Dual attitude of mental behaviour, denoted as 'Irupara Mana Iyal Parinamam' in Thamizh, and 'Dwapara Yugam' in Sanskrit ended, about 5,100 years ago.

In Evolution of Human, Bala Rama is denoted as the fourth stage and Lord Krishna as the fifth.

Regarding the 'Evolution of Life System', Bala Rama is termed the eighth and Lord Krisna as nine.

CHAPTER 23

Kali Yukham

After the end of 'The evolution of Dual Facets of mental attitude', and also after the Catastrophe, Kali Yukham commenced. After the advent of this Yuhkam, it is now 5,116th Year from Chitthirai 1, of Samvacchara year, and 14th April, 2014 A.D. as per Gregorian calendar.

Lord Krishna told Arjuna [Bhagavath Geetha] on Devotion and Salvation, thus:

"Some people take the path of telling my stories and try to reach me. (Salvation)

"Some take the path of listening to those stories and try to reach me.

"Some people decorate me* with wealth and ornaments, and thereby try to reach me. (*Idol Worship).

"Some people put their physic to suffering, and thereby try to reach Me.", and so on, and finally,

"Some try to know me through higher knowledge and try to reach me."

Lord Krishna himself took the path of higher knowledge and attained Eternity, as he revealed in Geetha that his 'was_the function enjoining the matured and cherished knowledge' (Kshetram, Kshetragnya Yogam).

Kali Yukham is based on the Evolution of knowledge and Science. The term, 'Kali' means the enablement of Kal. Kal - to dig/cull out the inner self of mind; kalvi-education -by culling out knowledge sprouts from within and spreads; Kalai- (kala +i-case ending) Branches of knowledge. Kalaacharam-perform/act based on the knowledge obtained within, i.e., culture.

The Core of Nature is denoted as 'Akaran'. Similarly, prime culture is denoted as Akara Kalaacharam, i.e., tilling the land and growing crops. In Sanskrit it is 'Agra Kalacharam', a phonetic variant of Thamizh word, and in English, 'Agriculture'. The man observed Nature and studied the seasons condusive to different agricultural operations, and, thereby, the time, date, and the cyclic operations as "year" was computed. Now, it is vivid that the knowledge has grown up like a Baniyan Tree with branches on various subjects, and has entwined into the life of every human. Unlike in the past, during this Yukham, i.e., Era, everyone can have access to the branch of his/her choice and aptitude, which has become the 'Religion of Life'.

Noble Laurate, Dr. Albert Einstein described on Religion and Science as below, in a Science held in 1937:

"Science without religion is lame. Religion without science is blind."

CHAPTER 24

Eleven (Urhutthirams) Reactions in nature.

In Thamizh, 'Urhum Thiram' denotes action, and its opposite term, 'Urhutthiram' denotes reaction. This term is denoted as 'Rudram' in Sanskrit, which is a phonetic variant of Thamizh word. When any activity, commences, Urhutthiram - Reaction manifests by nature.

There are eleven Urhutthirams in nature, which are detailed below. Along with Thamizh nomenclatures, Sanskrit and English terms are also furnished.

1) Kathiravanil irundu (From Sun)- **Karia Sivantha-Neela Kathirveechu.** Karia Sivantha –Red Rays embedded in core/hole, i.e., Infra Red Rays; Neela-Blue Rays; Kathir- Radioactive particles, and Kathir veechu-Radiation from the Radioactve particles. The blend of Red and Blue appears as Ootha shade (Violet). In this context these two colours are entwined and can be split, and as such, it is mentioned as 'Infra Red-Blue radiation'.

English: **Ultra Violet Rays from Sun.**

Sanskrit: **Sura Sreshta Neela Lohita Devah.** Sura –Radio active particles; Shresta-most important, Neela-Blue; Lohita devah- reddish Rays. Red and blue, Thamizh terms are juxtaposed. The Infra red is not depicted in true sense, and mentioned as Red.

2) **Nilaa- Vaama Thevam.** Nilaa-Moon; Vaama thevam- Rays can be understood by explanation and conceived by mind. This Refers to Umbra formed around moon during Solar Eclipse.

English: Umbra formed during Solar Eclipse.

Sanskrit: Nile Vaama Devah (as in Thamizh).

3. Thamizh: **Mukkan Asu - Neelan**. Mukkan Asu -Trivalent Oxygen, i.e., Ozone. Neelan- Blue colour.

English: Blue colour Rays spread in Ozone Layer by splitting Ultra Violet rays from sun.

Sanskrit: Asu- Neelah. Both the words are phonetic variants of Thamizh.

4. Thamizh:**Varunam in Puvanam**. Varunam -Ionisation/electrolysis. Puvanam- Ionosphere. Gases spread above atmosphere and below Ozone Layer cannot shrink due to cold, resulting in ionization as Anions (Thamizh- Peru Munai) and cations (Thamizh-Chayr Munai).

English: Ionosphere. Sanskrit: Buvaha.

5) Thamizh: **Vaanam- "Thatai"**. Vaanam - atmosphere; Thatai-blockade i.e., friction.

English: Friction in Atmosphere.

Sanskrit: Anthariksham- –Rithadhwajah. Antariksham - atmosphere; Rithadhwaja- blockade that rules.

6) Thamizh:**Puyalkatrin kanh.**(Puyalkatru–storm/Cyclone; kanh-Eye);

English: Eye of Storm.

Sanskrit: Aardoolam - Rudraksham.

[Note: A section of worshippers of Shiva denote that Eye of storm is the 'Third Eye' on the forehead of Shiva. His Weapon, Thrisoolam (trident), causes tri-ordial devastation, viz., Thunderstorms, heavy rains, and floods. The Serpants, viz., Thunderstorms, heavy rains, and floods. The Serpants, which he wears as his ornaments, are Whirlwinds (norwesters) and tornadoes, typhoons (twisters). They also term this "Eye of Storm" as "Rudhraaksha".

7) Thamizh: **Thee-Kozhunthu.**

English: Fire-flame

Sanskrit: Agni – Juhva (Juhva-Tongue).

8) Thamizh: **Neerchuzhal** il - Arru Madu

English: River – Gorge – Whirlpool.

Sanskrit- Nadhi- Ambi (also Jalakantah). His consort- Ambika

9) Thamizh- **Pittham.-Kuruthi Azhuttham**

English –Liver –Controls Blood pressure. (High blood Pressure leads to anger, and low blood pressure leads to fear and mental depression.)

Sanskrit–Manyu. (The word, as well as Rowdram (the one caused by Rudra – urutthiram, denotes anger.).

10) Thamizh -**Puvi – Erimalai – Kuzhambu.**

English –Volcano – Lava.

Sanskrit- Hataka Agni. Rudra manifest as Bhavaan and his consort –Bhavani.

11) Thamizh: **Mahki thalam.**

English: Hard Shell consisting mainly of Asbestos and Graphite -the stratum under Plates. This holds the Core of earth consisting of super heated ball of

metals under great pressure such that they cannot enlarge, melt, and flow out, protecting the Earth from devastating the Life System of Nature.
Sanskrit: Mahiyasan.

It is also stated that these eleven urutthirams (reactions) are in meditation and manifest on their own and set to react only when respective action commences.